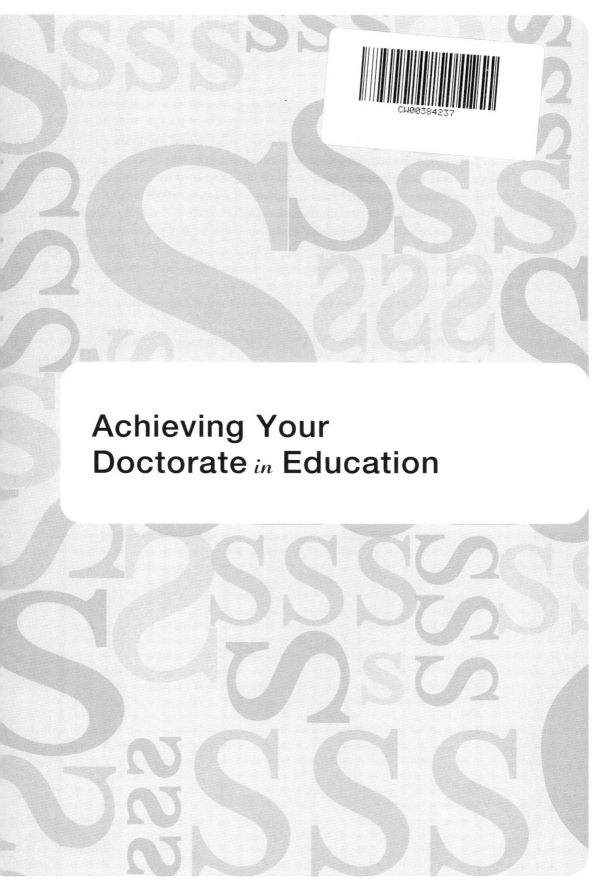

Achieving Your
Doctorate *in* Education

Achieving Your Doctorate in Education

This book is used on the Open University programme the Doctorate in Education (EdD). The EdD is a three-year programme of study. The first year centres on a literature review and initial research study. This is followed by a two-year programme of supported and supervised research that culminates in a 50,000 word thesis.

A growing number of professionals regard this style of doctoral programme as being a more appropriate vehicle for their further development than the traditional PhD. The programme has very specific entry criteria that include appropriate study at masters degree level that links to an EdD academic area of study and training in research skills and methods.

The OU EdD has been highly successful in terms of student completion and is a flourishing programme.

Details of this and other Open University courses can be obtained from the Student Registration and Enquiry Service, The Open University, PO Box 197, Milton Keynes MK7 6BJ, United Kingdom: tel. +44 (0)870 333 4340, e-mail general-enquiries@ open.ac.uk

Alternatively, you may visit the Open University website at http://www.open.ac.uk where you can learn more about the wide range of courses and packs offered at all levels by The Open University.

To purchase a selection of Open University course materials visit http://www.ouw. co.uk, or contact Open University Worldwide, Michael Young Building, Walton Hall, Milton Keynes MK7 6AA, United Kingdom for a brochure: tel. +44 (0)1908 858785; fax +44 (0)1908 858787; e-mail ouwenq@open.ac.uk

Study Skills

Achieving Your Doctorate
in Education

Hilary Burgess, Sandy Sieminski
and Lore Arthur

in association with

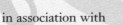

SAGE Publications
London • Thousand Oaks • New Delhi

SAGE Publications Ltd
1 Oliver's Yard
55 City Road
London EC1Y 1SP

SAGE Publications Inc.
2455 Teller Road
Thousand Oaks, California 91320

SAGE Publications India Pvt Ltd
B-42, Panchsheel Enclave
Post Box 4109
New Delhi 110 017

British Library Cataloguing in Publication data

A catalogue record for this book is available
from the British Library

ISBN-10 1-4129-1172-9   ISBN-13 978-1-4129-1172-6
ISBN-10 1-4129-1173-7   ISBN-13 978-1-4129-1173-3 (pbk)

Library of Congress Control Number: 2005934568

Typeset by C&M Digitals (P) Ltd., Chennai, India
Printed in Great Britain by Cromwell Press Ltd, Trowbridge, Wiltshire
Printed on paper from sustainable resources

Contents

Preface   vii

Author Biographies   ix

1   Choosing to do a Doctorate in Education   1

2   Organising and Planning Your Research   9

3   Developing a Literature Review   19

4   Ethics: Issues, Dilemmas and Problems   30

5   Developing Theoretical Frameworks   41

6   Methodological Considerations   52

7   Collecting Data   64

8   Analysing Data   80

9   The Writing Process   90

10 The Examining Process   102

11 Sharing Your Research Findings   115

Bibliography   123

Index   129

Preface

The Doctorate in Education (EdD) is the route to a doctoral qualification now chosen by many education professionals. This book is specifically oriented towards those studying for an EdD although it will have relevance for all who study for a professional doctorate. The origin of the book lies in our experiences of teaching students studying for EdD and other degrees and the issues and perspectives those students brought to educational research. It also originated in our shared view of the importance of research as an activity that should engage education professionals as they seek to extend their knowledge, skills, professionalism and develop evidence-based practice. It is not a research methods text book. There are a large number of 'how to do research' texts available and we refer to several in the following chapters that we think are particularly helpful. Possessing the right research skills is essential but that knowledge alone will not help you to achieve your doctorate. We are concerned with the issues linked to the processes of doing educational research that have particular relevance for our doctoral students. Some of these issues are closely linked to any doctoral research such as working with your supervisor, writing a literature review, developing a theoretical perspective, generating theory from data and the processes of writing up. Other issues are more specifically linked to doctorate in education students such as considering links to professional practice, reflection on knowledge and the growth of understanding among educational professionals.

Throughout the book the examples are drawn from the research and theses of students who have just completed their doctorates in education. The issues that we explore through these students, reveals that doing educational research is often a frustrating and messy business as well as an exciting process. We owe the students on the EdD programme at The Open University a huge debt of gratitude for allowing us to use their comments in electronic seminars, in course evaluations and in their theses as exemplars throughout the book. Many of the student comments remain anonymous but for those whose theses are referenced in the text, we would like to say a special word of thanks to Sophina Asong, Hazel Barnett, Lyndon Cabot, John Hamlin, Cheri Logan, Paul Redmond, Hazel Reid, Vivien Wilson, Lyn Karstadt, Paul Phillips, Jean Barnett, and Hilary Bennison. Their willingness to share your research experiences provides an invaluable contribution to the development of the professional knowledge and practicalities of doing research for a professional doctorate.

We have also benefited from our colleagues within The Open University and in other universities who read drafts, provided advice and contributed to the development of some of the chapters through providing material. In particular we would like to acknowledge Nigel Bennett, Gordon Bloomer, Bob Burgess, John Butcher, Marlene

Morrison, Martyn Hammersley, David Scott and Gina Wisker. In terms of book production we acknowledge the support of staff at The Open University and in particular Liz Kemp, who has since moved on but helped to set up the contract with Sage, and Gill Gowans and Emma Nugent who somehow managed to keep us all on track.

Finally, we would add that the views and comments expressed in this book are our own and any errors are entirely the responsibility of the authors.

Author Biographies

Hilary Burgess

Hilary Burgess is Director for Postgraduate Studies in the Centre for Research in Education and Educational Technology (CREET) at The Open University. She is also Chair of the Doctorate in Education Programme, Area Co-ordinator for Teacher Professional Development and Mentoring and an EdD supervisor. Her research and publications are in the areas of primary teaching and mentoring in primary and secondary schools. She joined The Open University in 1993 and initially worked as a PGCE Staff Tutor in the South Region. Previously, she was a Senior Lecturer in Primary Education at Westhill College in Birmingham and has taught in primary schools in Coventry and inner London.

Sandy Sieminski

Sandy Sieminski recently joined the Faculty of Health and Social Care at The Open University having previously worked as Staff Tutor for the Doctorate in Education programme. She began her career teaching on a range of Social Care courses and worked in a number of FE colleges. Sandy is a member of the Policy Making and Professionalism Research Group within CREET and has an interest in vocational education and training. Her research interests include the development of competence-based approaches to education and training. She has engaged in research that focuses on the implementation of NVQs and GNVQs and policy-making processes.

Lore Arthur

Lore Arthur is a Senior Lecturer in the Faculty of Education and Language Studies and Chair of the Masters Module Supporting Lifelong Learning at The Open University. She is also Area Co-ordinator and Research Supervisor for Lifelong Learning on the Doctorate in Education (EdD) programme at The Open University. Her research and publications are in the areas of lifelong learning, comparative and intercultural adult education. She joined The Open University in 1995. Previously, she was a Lecturer in Adult Education/Languages at Goldsmiths College, University of London for a number of years.

1 Choosing to do a Doctorate in Education

Choosing to study for a professional doctorate is a major decision and, for many, it is often the first step of a journey towards building and extending skills and knowledge about educational enquiry. It is a research journey that will allow you to pursue an area of personal interest and a research investigation in depth and in a way that you will not have had the opportunity to do before. Conducting your own research can be both exciting and rewarding as you uncover new ways of looking at events in educational settings or thinking about theoretical perspectives. As well as many highs during the process of your research there will also be some lows, and knowing how to manage your research throughout each different phase will help you to achieve your goal of a doctorate in education (EdD). There are a number of different issues to consider, as you will discover in later chapters, but we will begin by asking a question. Why do research for an EdD? Why is this an appropriate route for you rather than some other kind of higher degree such as a PhD? There are no doubt several reasons why you have selected this route to your doctorate. Whatever those reasons may be, it is relevant to know what lies behind gaining a doctoral qualification. In this chapter we will cover:

- **the professional doctorate and the EdD;**

- **why do an EdD?**

- **key issues – knowledge, the practitioner and reflection on practice.**

A brief explanation about the emergence of the professional doctorate, including the EdD, will provide some context.

The professional doctorate and the EdD

Professional doctorates in the UK emerged for a variety of reasons, depending on the subject area. For example, the engineering doctorate (EngD) was promoted by the Engineering and Physical Sciences Research Council (EPSRC) and developed to provide a high status route for young engineers pursuing industrial careers; the business doctorate (DBA) grew out of the highly successful MBA as a means to extend professional development further. The education doctorate developed through the initiatives of universities rather than a professional body or research council. As a consequence, the structure and length of EdD programmes may vary considerably, with some having more restrictive entrance requirements than others and often varying in length from 3 to 7 years. A majority of professional doctorates, including the EdD, are studied part-time. The UK Council for Graduate Education (UKCGE) notes that the EdD 'has developed to bring a demonstrably high level of research enquiry to bear within a practical context. This route is particularly relevant for experienced education professionals and is almost invariably undertaken on a part-time basis' (UKCGE 2002: 19).

The Economic and Social Research Council (ESRC) has recognised the relevance of the professional doctorate for educational practitioners and welcomed the development of such programmes in universities. The *Postgraduate Training Guidelines* (ESRC 2005) now include a section of guidance for the professional doctorate (termed PD) where it is described as an exciting innovation within the field of doctoral study. The term 'professional doctorate' incorporates the range of doctorates in the UK, including the DBA in the field of business and management and the DClinPsy or DEdPsy in psychology as well as the EdD. A distinguishing feature of a professional doctorate is the undertaking of an original piece of research and, therefore, a grasp of research methods is required. The ESRC state: 'Professional doctorates aim to develop an individual's professional practice and to support them in producing a contribution to [professional] knowledge' (ESRC 2005: 93).

While the development of professional knowledge is seen as particularly important within an EdD, a number of other features are identified by the ESRC. For example, the requirement of an independent piece of research expected to include 'real-life' issues concerned with practice, and an expectation that close interaction with professionally related problems would lead to opportunities for personal and professional development through the processes of research. It is suggested that research training should include a range of methodological approaches. The way in which the professional doctorate provides a link between theory and practice and how the overall pedagogical philosophy underlying the doctorate supports students during their research are considered by the ESRC to be key issues for all professional doctorate programmes.

The EdD, therefore, is a professionally-oriented doctorate that allows professionals to develop and refine their research skills, to carry out a substantial piece of research and to reflect upon their own practice. This is often indicated in the prospectuses of those universities who offer the EdD and such documentation normally makes explicit the aim of linking professional practice, professional knowledge and research. For example, one university prospectus states that the EdD is:

An innovative programme designed for professionals in education and related areas who want to extend and deepen their knowledge and understanding of contemporary educational issues. It is characterised by a substantial taught element and a modular structure. It aims to develop skills in research and enquiry and to use these in order to carry out research that will contribute to professional knowledge and practice. A growing number of professionals regard this style of doctoral programme as being a more appropriate vehicle for their further development than the traditional PhD.

(Open University 2004: 19)

A wide range of professionals are attracted to study a doctorate in education, from primary and secondary schoolteachers to heads of further education colleges and staff in university departments. In addition, those who work in educational administration or in local education authorities may embark upon an education doctorate. Very often, the EdD student population will include professionals from related fields such as medicine and social work. Students on EdD programmes come from very diffuse backgrounds, and one of the issues that the professional doctorate in education has had to contend with is how to create a recognisable identity and a coherent structure that will support the variety and range of research topics such a body of students will choose to follow. For many programmes, that coherence is achieved through a modular structure with a taught element embedded in the course. The taught element ensures that the part-time doctoral students engage in regular dialogue with their supervisors and a community of other student researchers, allowing them to reflect on their own progress and avoid the feelings of isolation that have, until recent years, been associated with part-time PhD study. The perceived nature of the EdD as a manageable, structured route to a doctorate is essential for many who study by this means, as one EdD graduate indicated in an anonymous evaluation at the end of an EdD programme:

The process of submitting assignments on a regular basis was essential. The EdD is very focused because of the word limit. Having to work to deadlines suited my lifestyle and meant that work was completed in the allotted time.

The structure and support which helped me stay on track whilst holding down a job that takes me all over the country is quite difficult to balance without that underlying structure.

(EdD Graduate 2004)

As evidenced by the comment above, the taught element of the EdD is particularly important to students. The structure supported by the completion of regular assignments appeals to busy professionals working full-time who want to research their own practice.

Why do an EdD?

Taking the decision to register for a doctoral programme is a huge step. It requires a vast commitment to several years of research and study, giving up other activities and hobbies, and very often giving up much of a social life until it is completed. So what is the motivation for those who decide to follow this route? For some, the EdD is seen as a pathway to being involved in doing research that has personal professional relevance and is applicable to real-life educational practice. As one EdD graduate has remarked:

> *I would never have embarked on or completed a PhD. I am ideologically opposed to research into an esoteric area of study that has no application to the 'real' world.*

(EdD Graduate 2004)

Some choose to do a doctorate in education because it appears more manageable in terms of completion and for those who are mid-career professionals this can be a key issue.

> *I have many colleagues who have begun a part-time PhD. Most have given up along the way.*

(EdD Graduate 2004)

Many students undertake an EdD, not because they wish to further their careers, but simply because they have a curiosity and interest in an aspect of their own work that they would like to investigate further. They would like to develop and extend their professional knowledge and undertaking an EdD provides the opportunity to do so. The aim is to know more about something at the end of the process than you do at the beginning. Pole and Lampard (2002) suggest that when research is reduced to very simple characteristics it cuts away the mystique that can sometimes surround it and focuses upon the actual processes of doing it. From simple beginnings it is possible to build up to more complex questions about the nature of educational research that you would like to undertake and the relationship between the research question, the research methods and the generation of knowledge through data. Right from the beginning of your research you will need to think about some of the key issues that it will be important to address if you are to achieve your doctorate successfully.

Key issues – knowledge, the practitioner and reflection on practice

There are many factors that will contribute to you gaining your EdD and to some extent these will vary from other EdD participants depending upon your personal and work circumstances. Some issues, however, will be present for all, although how you might resolve them will be different. In this book we have devoted individual chapters to some of the key issues, such as managing your time and your supervisor, getting to grips with your literature review, developing a theoretical perspective, analysing and collecting data, ethical issues and the writing process. Throughout each of the chapters threads of our central themes are used to link together the processes of doing research.

These themes may well be central to all doctoral programmes, such as contributing to knowledge, linking the academic and the professional, developing a rigorous approach to your research, reflection upon the research processes and reflection upon practice.

As an educational practitioner entering an EdD programme you will find that you have much to offer in terms of your previous academic study and work experience as well as much to learn. It is important, as Pole and Lampard (2002: 5) suggest, to pose a number of questions about your proposed research:

1   **Why am I doing this research?**

2   **What is the need for this research?**

3   **Where will the research lead?**

4   **What are the issues I wish to address and/or the debates to which I wish to contribute?**

While these are simple questions that you may have already begun to think about if you have had to write a proposal to gain entrance to your EdD programme, they are worth keeping in mind throughout the various processes of your research. Such questions help to keep you focused and continually explaining to yourself what it is that you are trying to investigate. A clear rationale about why you want to do your research and where you hope it will lead will help to keep you motivated and moving forward in your research studies. It will also help you to refine your professional knowledge as you make links between your workplace setting and the assignments or progress reports that you are required to undertake for your doctorate. Scott et al. (2004) have argued that on EdD programmes the relationship between course content and practice is ambiguous, uncertain or implicit. They suggest that the relationship between programme content and professional practice therefore emerges through written assignments or personal reflection and informal discussion. While the connection between practitioner experience and an EdD programme may occur implicitly, there is often great value to be gained by individual students from working in this way, as one EdD graduate revealed in an end-of-course evaluation:

> *The EdD is closely related to practice and the link between theory and practice. Study complemented my professional role, both informing the other. Research findings were immediately applicable to my day-to-day work.*

(EdD Graduate 2004)

A carefully chosen topic linked to a workplace setting can greatly enhance the knowledge of a practitioner and provide a means for improving practice. Researching your topic will allow you the opportunity to reflect upon your role in your workplace and may well bring to the surface issues that you were only vaguely aware of in your daily routine. One of the principal aims of a professional doctorate is the development of the reflective practitioner (Scott et al. 2004). Such reflection is not necessarily about improving practice, particularly when many doctoral students are at a stage in their careers where they are already highly experienced practitioners, but rather it is about gaining a deeper and more profound understanding of the practice setting. Two EdD graduates give their views of the reflective processes at work in an EdD programme:

> *It has led to greater reflection on learning processes, linking theory to practice and seeing the two as inseparable.*

> *I believe I am developing an ability to reflect critically on my own work. In particular I am building on work studied on the MA course on critical self-reflection and the 'reflective practitioner' in reflecting on the shortcomings and strengths of the methodology used.*

(EdD Gradutes 2004)

In the above examples, reflection is evident in a number of different ways. The first example shows how one EdD student is able to focus on learning processes and move between the workplace and academic study making connections between the two. For this student, the reflective processes led to theory and practice merging into being 'insep-arable'. The second graduate used reflection as a means to develop skill as a researcher through focusing upon the methodology used in her study and she felt a connection between her earlier studies and current research as an EdD student. Reflection allowed these students to develop procedural and technical knowledge. Procedural knowledge is described by Wenger (1998) as the characteristics of a community of practice (see Lave and Wenger 1991). Dependency relationships established within a community result in developing shared practice that has specific forms of communication that may not be evident to an outsider. Learning processes in an educational setting may well have such 'shared practices' embedded within their design and structure. Technical knowledge is described by Shulman (1987) as those areas of knowledge that practitioners need to be acquainted with in order to carry out their job effectively. These areas span content knowledge, pedagogical knowledge, principles and strategies of management and organ-isation, curriculum knowledge, knowledge of learners, knowledge of educational con-texts and knowledge of educational purposes and values. The development of such practical professional knowledge through reflection on educational practice can also lead to new areas of research study, as another EdD graduate revealed.

> *As my research heads towards a conclusion I am increasingly confident, having extensively reviewed the literature, that this is a unique piece of research. It will be of interest to serving Heads ... but it should also be of relevance to a wider audience with new, albeit limited insight into understanding how a Head's autonomy is perceived to impact on a school's effectiveness.*

(EdD Graduate 2004)

In this case reflection led to an understanding of the uniqueness of the research undertaken.

The issue of originality within an EdD thesis is one that both students and examiners have tussled with in the past. How do you know that your research is original or of significance? Some EdD programmes may have criteria for assessing theses that require a significant contribution to the theory and practice of education. Views on originality and significance may be wide-ranging and one group of examiners, at The Open University, in an institutional exercise to standardise and moderate their use of marking criteria, suggested the following:

Criteria 2: 'makes a significant contribution to the theory and practice of education'

The majority of examiners agreed that a thesis that fulfils this criteria:

- *Could realistically be used to shape future research or practice at a national, or more likely, local level.*
- *Presents rich sources of data and indicates areas for further research.*
- *A 'significant contribution' entails the criteria of originality and relevance. It is demonstrated by evidence of advancing professional knowledge and understanding of the theory and practice of education at an individual, institutional or national/global level.*
- *Is of interest to other professionals working in the field.*
- *Is of publishable quality.*

(OU Co-ordination Exercise 2003)

These criteria identified by the examiners reveal some of the tension between the professional and theoretical aspects surrounding studying for an EdD. Research for an EdD thesis is usually small and local so the contribution is likely to be most relevant to that local setting and it may not be possible to generalise much from the findings. The examiners argue, however, that the contribution should link to earlier research and may give insights relevant to the local setting which are new or innovative.

The growth of professional knowledge through reflection on practice will, therefore, be a central part of your developing EdD thesis. That reflection will be linked to both your workplace setting and your developing academic knowledge. It will be the processes of doing your research that will enable such reflection and that may lead you in new directions in the future, as one EdD graduate commented:

I now understand my role as [Head of Department] better and can see the flaws in the senior management of the school ... the way I will manage my department will be different, as will the way I will introduce innovation and deal with members of my team.

(EdD Graduate 2004)

There are many changes that can flow from undertaking a piece of doctoral research, whether it is gaining a better understanding of workplace roles, or dealing with management and innovation. One thing is certain when you start your research for your EdD. The processes you will undergo as you carry out your doctoral research will lead to many changes in your life and work as you reflect, research and study.

Conclusion

In this chapter we have tried to convey what is distinctive about studying for an EdD in the context of a wide variety of other professional doctorates. We have explored reasons why professionals study for an EdD and some of the benefits they have gained from doing so. In identifying some key issues that we consider have relevance for all those who undertake a professional doctorate, we hope that you will continue to revisit ideas surrounding professional knowledge and practice and reflection on practice as you study. In the next chapter we explore organising and planning your research.

Research is an engaging and all-consuming activity and once you have achieved your doctorate you may find it hard to let go! We hope the advice in the following chapters will help to support you on your journey towards achieving your EdD and becoming a competent researcher in the process.

2 Organising and Planning Your Research

Completing a doctorate in education while engaged in a demanding professional role is an exciting challenge for the busy educational professional. The highly structured nature of EdD programmes, which entails the regular submission of assignments that contribute in some way to the production of the finished thesis, makes this an increasingly popular choice for professionals working in higher education and in a range of educational contexts. The production of a thesis may be the longest piece of continuous writing that you have ever undertaken. New research techniques will need to be acquired but you will be able to draw upon the many skills and understandings developed through prior academic study. Your research experiences will cover a wide range of feelings, from excitement to periods of frustration. A supervisor plays a key role in helping you remain motivated and focused through the highs and lows that you may encounter as you engage in your study. In this chapter we consider ways of making the most of the support available to you throughout your journey.

This chapter covers:

- **developing your research proposal;**

- **the role of the supervisor;**

- **working effectively with your supervisor;**

- **supervision sessions;**

- **managing time;**

- **linking up with other researchers.**

Developing your research proposal

Several EdD programmes will ask applicants to submit a research proposal as a part of the application process. Some institutions may include the development of a proposal as a part of an EdD programme. In one of your early meetings with your allocated supervisor(s) you will no doubt revisit your initial proposal in order to refine the focus and design of your research. One of the issues that supervisors frequently have to help students with is that the research proposed is often too broad. The supervisor will discuss ways of refining the initial area with you so that the proposed project is feasible within an acceptable time-frame. An experienced Open University EdD supervisor, whom we have called 'Ellen', reflected on her work with different students and identified a number of ways in which students' initial ideas needed rethinking in the context of their professional roles:

> *The first thing that I often have to address with EdD students is the scale of their proposed research project. Sometimes the proposed area of focus is too big and not thought through in terms of reality. For example, Terry had an interesting project. He was interested in teaching and learning in science. It was initially a very broad proposal not based on one year group or class. He had mixed up gender issues, special needs issues and did not have a tight enough focus. There was no real research design. He would not have enough data to focus on any one innovation or thing.*

During Ellen's first meeting with Terry she had to help him consider the feasibility of his initial proposal by considering all the difficulties he might confront. The research proposal should contain an estimate of the time you intend to take to collect and analyse your data. You will need to consider whether your plans fit with your institution's timescale for EdD completion. For example, an Open University student normally spends three years preparing a thesis, after studying a research methods course. Typically, an EdD student will collect data during the second of the three years, and in the third year complete the data analysis and finish writing the thesis. Ellen needed to feel confident that Terry could undertake his proposed research within this time-frame. To support Terry effectively, Ellen felt that she needed to consider the professional context in which Terry worked and explore access to data and ethical issues surrounding his proposed study. Gaining access to sites for research may be a complicated business and, as Delamont et al. (1997) note, many novice researchers are caught out by the length of time negotiating access can take.

For Ellen, understanding where a student is coming from is very important because appreciating this helps her to provide support successfully. She explains:

> *When I meet the student I try to find out what makes them tick and I need to understand their professional position. The most successful students tie their research into their work. We explore how the thesis ties in with their workload. This then helps the student to refine their initial ideas in terms of feasibility.*

The benefit of engaging in a dialogue with your supervisor about your proposed research is that during such discussion ways of refining the design and issues that may complicate the research process can be explored. Although it is anticipated that this will be the focus of an early supervision session, it is something that you are likely to need to consider at various points during your period of study, as you acquire relevant new knowledge and understanding of your area of interest. The research proposal is a useful foundation from which to develop your ideas and arguments and initially it can be viewed as a draft outline that can be worked with in a dynamic way in the future. Periodically re-examining your proposal throughout the research process, and considering how your thinking has shifted with respect to different aspects of your research, is a valuable activity in which to engage. One way of doing this is to ask yourself various questions about your research and make notes on how far and why your thinking has changed:

- **What is/are my research question(s)?**

- **What are the ethical issues I need to consider?**

- **What relevant investigations and findings have been carried out by other researchers?**

- **How does my research build on the work of other researchers interested in the area I intend to focus on?**

- **What are the main conceptual frameworks and theories that are likely to aid my analysis of data?**

- **What justification can I offer for my choice of research strategy and methods of data collection?**

- **When will data collection and analysis take place?**

The role of the supervisor

The supervisor with whom you work will be an experienced academic with expertise in the field of research that you have chosen to focus on. It may well be the case that the supervisor does not possess expertise in all aspects of the research student's proposed study; therefore every university will have arrangements in place to support supervisors in their work either through a system of a second supervisor or the presence of a supervisory team. Supervision arrangements will vary depending on the structures for student support that exist within institutions. However, the Quality Assurance Agency for Higher Education *Code of Practice for the Assurance of Academic Quality and Standards in Higher Education* (QAA 2004) will have a bearing on arrangements for postgraduate supervision. Higher education institutions will need to ensure that they have systematic and clear supervision arrangements in place that allow for regular and appropriate supervisory support. Within the *Code of Practice*, emphasis is placed on the value of a supervisory team approach to support postgraduate research. The QAA

(2004) documentation notes that even where students have one main supervisor this person will normally be part of a supervisory team. The advantages of a team approach to student support are highlighted in the *Code of Practice*:

> *A supervisory team can give the student access to a multi-faceted support network, which may include: other research staff and students in the subject; a departmental adviser to postgraduate students; a faculty postgraduate tutor, or other individuals in similar roles.*
>
> *Between them the main supervisor and, where appropriate, other members of the supervisory team, will ensure that research students receive sufficient support and guidance to facilitate their success.*
>
> *At least one member of the supervisory team will be currently engaged in research in the relevant discipline(s), so as to ensure that the direction and monitoring of the student's progress is informed by up-to-date subject knowledge and research developments.*
>
> *Breadth of experience and knowledge across the supervisory team will mean that the student always has access to someone with experience of supporting research students(s) through successful completion of their programme.*

(QAA 2004: 14–15)

You should familiarise yourself with the arrangements for supervision and support that exist within your institution and the regulations which outline the roles and responsibilities of both supervisors and students. It is important to know how different members of staff can support you with your research.

Essentially, the supervisor can be seen as a critical friend whose role entails providing guidance about the feasibility and manageability of the proposed research that will help with the development of your research proposal. The supervisor will be able to provide advice about methodological and ethical issues that are important to consider, data collection and analysis, the writing up of the thesis, and preparation for the viva voce examination. The supervisor will, inevitably, have an important role to play in checking academic arguments and the validity of the claims made in your thesis. He or she will also have a role to play in monitoring your progress and helping to identify suitable external examiners. Throughout your period of registration for the degree the supervisor will play a key role in helping to keep you focused and motivated so that you are successful in achieving your EdD.

At the beginning of the research process you are likely to be fairly dependent on your supervisor's guidance, but as your work progresses you will naturally develop a greater degree of autonomy. As time goes by, you will develop expertise in your chosen area of study; indeed, it is to be expected that you will eventually have greater knowledge of your chosen field than your supervisor. Research undertaken by Delamont et al. (1997) reveals how the relationship between the student and supervisor changes over time. They note a shift in the degree of dependence and subordination of the student in relation to their supervisor as they develop as researchers and they refer to this as an 'intellectual growing-up'. As you develop as a researcher your needs will change and this may entail renegotiating the ground rules of the relationship you have with your supervisor.

Working effectively with your supervisor

Naturally, you will want to maintain a good working relationship with your supervisor throughout your period of study. In part, this is dependent on effective communication and keeping each other informed about changes in arrangements and agreements made regarding the submission of assignments and tutorial contact. Your supervisor will set aside time to respond to the work that you have submitted and if you cannot keep to an agreed schedule he or she will need to know in advance. It is important that you discuss how you will work together to avoid misunderstandings that may have a detrimental effect on your relationship.

Research undertaken by Phillips (1994) draws attention to the common problem of 'communications breakdown' between students and their supervisors. This can emerge when the perceptions of the student and the supervisor are at odds with each other. Phillips notes that a common cause of this problem arises because there are different expectations of the degree and frequency of supervision. A supervisor may feel frustrated by the high degree of dependency that a research student has on his or her guidance. Alternatively, a supervisor may feel that the student is making good progress and therefore believe that the most appropriate style of supervision is minimal interference but this may not be what the student feels is needed. In contrast to this, a student may be quite happy with limited supervisory contact. However, this may create a situation whereby the supervisor feels left in the dark and is not sure about the progress the student is making in periods between submission of compulsory assignments. One EdD student describes how his assumptions about the nature of the supervisory relationship were called into question:

> *The initial contact was positive and I was very pleased, if surprised, at the detailed feedback and the articles and references he sent me. I started to make good progress. However, what I did not realise was that my supervisor was slowly becoming increasingly worried and rather angry about my lack of communication between assignments. I did not feel that I was expected to be emailing or phoning my supervisor and, indeed, I did not want to 'bother him'. The first I realised that there was a problem was when out of the blue an email came from my supervisor saying that he was fed up with me and going to speak to the Postgraduate Research Tutor about being removed as my supervisor. My lack of contact had been interpreted as a lack of commitment to my research. I was completely shocked and saddened by this since as I say I had been very grateful for all he had done for me. I spoke to my supervisor to try to resolve the issue and we came to an agreement that we would send weekly reports copied into the Postgraduate Research Tutor until his confidence in me was restored. That has continued to this day and although to be honest it is a real pain at times, for example when I have been away from work and have very little to say, it has kept me focused and his confidence is I think now restored.*

(EdD Graduate 2004)

Relationships between students and supervisors need to be based on clear expectations. Delamont et al. (1997) suggest that problems that occur in relation to supervision arrangements stem essentially from a failure to set out the expectations both parties have for the relationship. One strategy for managing supervision effectively and avoiding misunderstandings is to draw up a learning contract with your supervisor. This document does not have to be set in stone as it is difficult to predict the kinds of support that you will require at the outset, but it can provide a useful point of reference for both you and your supervisor. Wisker (2001) advocates the use of such a document to ensure clarity. The learning contract can make expectations explicit. For example, it may state the frequency of contact, the expected behaviours of the student and the supervisor and the kinds of support the supervisor feels able to offer. In addition to clarifying roles and expectations, the document also serves to help you identify transparent goals and outcomes, with a clear idea of how you intend to achieve them.

If things start to go wrong

Throughout the research process there are always periods of emotional highs and lows. It is a good idea to share any anxiety you have about your work with your supervisor so that he or she can offer constructive and supportive advice. There are occasions when the working relationship between a supervisor and student breaks down, and it is better to work with another person and establish a new working relationship than try to work in an unsatisfactory situation. However, as Phillips and Pugh (2000) note, it can be a difficult situation to work through as they suggest that:

> A change of supervisors is the academic equivalent of getting a divorce. There are the formal (legal) mechanisms for doing it but the results are achieved, inevitably, only after considerable emotional upset. There are important consequences for the supervisor's professional status and self-esteem if a student initiates a change. Thus it is bound to be a difficult process – often ending with metaphorical blood on the walls.

(Phillips and Pugh 2000: 113)

One way to reduce the emotional turmoil that you and your supervisor may experience as a result of requesting a change of supervisor is to involve a third party as a mediator in the discussion about this. Every institution will have a member of staff who has responsibility for research students on a particular programme, such as the EdD or other postgraduate study, who will have experience of supporting research students and supervisors when tensions emerge in their relationship. The person who plays this third-party role may be able to help you and your supervisor to identify exactly what the fundamental cause of the problem is and where possible to discuss this with a view to resolving the problems you are facing.

Supervision sessions

Throughout your period of study there will be opportunities for you to have supervision sessions. Institutional arrangements for support will vary from one institution to another so it is important to find out how many hours have been allocated for supervision in each academic year. Then you can plan to use this time as fruitfully as possible. It is important to discuss with your supervisor ways of making supervision opportunities effective and efficient.

For email supervision sessions, it is useful to make a list of concise points that you would like to explore during supervision. You may want to agree with your supervisor the time slot within which the supervision will run. This may well extend over a couple of days, with perhaps two or three exchanges from each of you at different points during that period.

You may find it helpful to precede planned telephone supervision with some emailed questions and/or an agenda or points on which you would welcome discussion and guidance. An example of an agenda for this kind of supervision is shown in the box.

Dear Sue,

Thank you for your recent feedback on my last assignment. I know we have agreed to have a telephone tutorial at 7p.m. next week. I have sketched out an agenda and you may have things to add. I will send you my notes from my latest reading on intensification so that you can see where I am with my understanding of issues.

Looking forward to speaking to you,

Sally

Telephone tutorial agenda

1. To go through the feedback provided on my last assignment – checking my understanding of what I need to do.
2. To consider some of the key issues for my research arising from my reading of the literature relating to the intensification of teachers' work.
3. To discuss the use of the concept on alienation in my data analysis.
4. To discuss a practical timetable for completion of new work that will be part of my assignment.

Having sent off your agenda, your supervisor will then be in a better position to respond in an informed way when you come to speak on the telephone, and this should help to maximise the benefits to be gained from the interaction. After the telephone supervision session has ended, try to construct a record of the advice given during your discussion.

Keeping a record of advice given during supervision is important as you may feel, especially in the early phases of your research, that a range of ideas have been explored that you find overwhelming. You will need to consider the relevance and practicalities of suggestions made by your supervisor and seek clarification where necessary. You may also wish to consider providing your supervisor with a record of your understanding of the advice given, which can be done by email if this is the most convenient medium for you both, to ensure that you are both clear about the proposed course of action that results from the session.

Remember that it is your responsibility to initiate discussions and negotiate agendas with your supervisor. Your supervisor will want you to succeed and it is important that you both feel you are working constructively together.

Dealing with feedback

The assignments that you produce during your EdD are likely to contribute to the production of your final thesis. For example, Open University EdD students complete eleven assignments over a three-year period, and during the first two years these all focus on different aspects of their research. In the first year students undertake a literature review and later assignments focus on research methods, data analysis and the presentation of findings. The feedback students receive on their assignments can be used for revising their work for presentation as chapters in the completed thesis.

Your supervisor will provide you with comprehensive feedback on each of the assignments that you submit. A supervisor should give feedback in writing as this will provide you with insight into what he or she is looking for and will help with the setting of writing goals for your next assignment or section of your thesis. You may find that, as well as noting the strengths of the work you have submitted, some of the comments are critical of certain aspects of your work. As an experienced research supervisor, Cryer (1996) is aware that feedback which is perceived by students as negative can at times provoke distressing emotions. Her advice in relation to this is helpful and reminds us that how we are feeling is quite normal during the production of a thesis:

> *Start by accepting that certain emotions are normal. You may be embarrassed at what you think your supervisor is seeing as your inadequacy and you may be angry at how he or she appears to misunderstand you. Understandable as these emotions are, it is counter-productive to let them show, and the chances are that, when you calm down, you will realise that they were unjustified anyway.*

(Cryer 1996: 66)

In such circumstances, Cryer suggests that it is helpful to consider the effort that the supervisor has put into preparing detailed feedback. However, it is your thesis and you will know the implications for your own work and the situation you are in. You may need time to reflect on what has been said and possibly seek clarification for points made and then engage in further discussion. It is worth bearing in mind that critical commentary on your work may be disheartening at first but when you read your supervisor's feedback carefully you will see how their advice may pave the way for greater creativity. As one Open University EdD graduate noted in the end-of-course evaluation questionnaire, the feelings of disappointment about work produced are not an uncommon experience for research students but he suggests they need to move beyond this and recognise the value of the comments made:

> *Getting a piece back with objections from your supervisor can, once the initial disappointment is over, be the start of a fantastic new development in your thinking. It is that dialogue between you and your supervisor that should provide the catalyst for your thesis to come alive, so embrace it.*

(EdD Graduate 2004)

Managing time

By looking ahead at the submission dates for assignments, you may well identify competing demands at various points in the year. You will need to plan ahead and think carefully about managing your time to avoid feeling overwhelmed by these competing demands. Ideally, you will want to create a balance between your studies, professional responsibilities and your personal life.

It is advisable to set timescales for the completion of the thesis and the key stages in that process. It is important to bear in mind that some parts of the research may take longer than anticipated. Naturally, you will want to estimate how much time you need to set aside for activities leading up to the submission of the various assignments you must produce, and try to identify time slots when you will be able to engage in these. One strategy for doing this is to look towards the goals set for a given period of time and to work backwards, considering the tasks to be completed successfully to achieve the objectives identified.

When it comes to the period in which you start to write up your research, the timescale can be open-ended, and it is easy for this period to lack focus and to take longer than necessary. It is therefore useful to prepare a timetable of activity and share this with your supervisor so that he or she can comment on the feasibility. This will help to keep you motivated and on task with your research.

Linking up with other researchers

During the course of your research you will want to obtain advice from other people, and many institutions will provide opportunities to interact with other researchers. There may be electronic conferences and email systems to encourage and facilitate this kind of interaction. Engaging in such networks can help to overcome feelings of isolation that you may experience as a part-time student. Inevitably, contact with other students, especially those researching in areas related to your own study, are likely to prove extremely valuable.

Conclusion

In this chapter we have stressed the importance of establishing a good working relationship with your supervisor and reaching an agreement about how you work together. Supervisors have a wealth of experience and can offer advice on the feasibility and design of your proposed research. Keeping a record of advice given by your supervisor will be helpful to refer to as you develop your thesis. Constructing a realistic timetable for producing work will help to keep your research on track.

In the next chapter we will look at developing a literature review. As you become increasingly familiar with the literature that relates to your research study you will be able to refine your research questions or the problems that you want to address.

3 Developing a Literature Review

Undertaking a critical review of the relevant literature sounds very grand and possibly a little daunting for a novice researcher, especially the idea of critically reviewing the work of established academics in the field. But a literature review entails more than a critical appraisal of the work of other researchers and, in fact, such commentary may form only a part of the discussion. A literature review provides a means of grounding your research and explaining its relevance. As you identify, review and relate the literature to your own research there are a number of important issues to consider which will help to clarify what is involved in preparing a literature review. In this chapter we focus on the development of a literature review by considering:

- **the purpose of a literature review;**

- **the character of different forms of literature;**

- **strategies for recording key points made in the literature;**

- **developing academic writing skills;**

- **developing an argument;**

- **the assessment of your literature review.**

A major task you will need to undertake for your EdD is to conduct a search of the published literature in your chosen research area and to undertake a critical review of it. The way in which you construct your literature review may vary depending on your institution's conventions about its presentation within the thesis. The literature review may be integrated throughout the thesis and carefully related to each section. Alternatively, it may be presented as an early chapter which provides a coherent synthesis of past and present research that relates clearly to the area of investigation, and offers a justification for the research reported and analysed in the thesis. If this approach is taken you will still need to demonstrate your knowledge and understanding not just in the literature review chapter but across all parts of your thesis.

The literature review involves, in part, a development of the reading that you carried out when preparing your research proposal. Throughout the period of registration for your EdD your familiarity with and understanding of the literature will grow. Your search and review of the literature should also enable you to refine, and perhaps reformulate, the questions that you posed at the outset, and even identify new ones that can be incorporated into your developing plans. While it is important not to be overawed by the literature, it is also essential to ensure, as far as possible, that the answers to the questions that you want to research are not already known and that your work builds upon and extends research already done. Eventually you will need to show where your research fits into the body of knowledge of which it is a part. In doing this it is important to bear in mind that doctoral research is very rarely completely new and original. Rather, it is generally concerned with making an additional (and probably relatively small) contribution to an existing body of knowledge. Sometimes it may simply extend that knowledge by using a new population, broadening or deepening what is known or extending the timescale. Sometimes it may use a new methodology to confirm – or possibly challenge – previous research findings.

At the beginning of your literature search it is wise to be fairly open-minded in considering anything that may have relevance to your study. However, it is important to be aware of the danger of falling into the trap of devoting too much time to searching for literature rather than reflecting on it and critically engaging with it; in fact, there is a danger that the search can become a displacement activity which distracts you from the task at hand. As you survey the literature for your research it is important to keep in mind what you are attempting to investigate and the relationship of the literature to your area of interest. As your work progresses, the relevance of the literature you are familiar with will become clearer alongside the clarification and development of your ideas about your research topic. Your judgement about the relevance will change over time, as the shape of your investigation sharpens. This is not something that will be accomplished at the beginning of your work, but will continue throughout the process of your research. Constructing a literature review is not a discrete task and you do not need to feel that you have found all the relevant literature before moving on to carry out your research. Throughout your period of registration you will be consulting literature to enhance your understanding and to strengthen various aspects of the research process.

The literature that you identify for possible inclusion in your review may be relevant not only because of the area of focus, but because the authors' methodology relates to your work or, for example, the concepts employed by authors in their data analysis may be helpful for you to draw upon or adapt for your own purposes. As your focus sharpens you will be able to be more selective in your use of the literature. As you start to integrate the literature into your research study, difficult decisions will have to be made about what to include and, as Bell (1999) notes:

It may well be that a great deal of what has been read will need to be abandoned when the review is prepared. What at one stage might have seemed to be a promising line of enquiry may prove to be of little use once more reading has been done. A hundred, or even a thousand individual pieces of information may emerge and be interesting in their own right but it is only when they are grouped, balanced against other findings and presented in a way readers can understand, that you have a review which is coherent and which has avoided the 'furniture sales catalogue' approach.

(Bell 1999: 98)

In making choices about the inclusion of various sources of literature, it is important to bear in mind what kinds of purposes a literature review can serve. Bruce (1994) explored postgraduate research students' understandings of the term 'literature review' and the meaning of a literature review for their research. Her findings led her to suggest that during the early stages of the research process it may be conceived by students as a listing of pertinent literature, or as a search for information and as a survey for the discipline's knowledge base. While these activities may prove to be a useful starting point for developing a literature review, Bruce argues:

Students' thinking needs to be challenged as early as possible in their research programme so that it is clear that the final product of the literature review is a coherent synthesis of past and present research. It is not a list or annotated bibliography on the area of interest.

(Bruce 1994: 210)

The purpose of a literature review

For the EdD student, the literature review can serve different purposes at particular stages in the research process. Some of the purposes listed below have more in keeping with the 'search' and 'survey' conceptions identified by Bruce (1994) during the early stages of postgraduate students' research. The final review that EdD students need to produce will entail critical evaluation of the literature that they have drawn on for their research. The list offered below highlights some important functions that the literature review can serve. Nevertheless, you may have additional purposes that you would wish to include.

- **To help you to identify information that is useful for your own research.**

- **To enable you to identify gaps in the knowledge about the area that you have chosen to focus on.**

- **To help you to clarify and refine your research questions or the problem that you want to address by considering related research findings.**

- **To serve as a sounding board to check out your ideas about your project.**

- **To enable you to make comparisons with other research and draw together perspectives on themes and topics.**

- **To help you to identify an appropriate research methodology for your investigation.**

- **To help you to devise conceptual and theoretical frameworks that can be used for the collection and analysis of data by considering how other researchers have focused on an area/issue.**

- **To demonstrate your familiarity with the subject area that you have chosen to investigate, by providing an overview of previous investigations.**

- **To compare your results with those of others to show how and where your contribution has taken place.**

- **To identify perspectives and findings that can be used to support and refute the arguments that you make in your thesis.**

- **To be able to construct a justification for the focus of your research and the way that you have carried it out.**

The variety of purposes that a literature review can serve will change as you progress with your research. For example, in the early stages of your research you may simply be interested in understanding the results of a piece of work. Critically appraising the work of others can be a challenging task for the novice researcher but by doing so you will generate ideas for developing your own work. As you read through the literature you will start to identify where there are gaps in the knowledge with regard to particular issues, and be able to consider how your study will be able to make a contribution to advancing understanding.

As your research develops, your reading of the literature may influence your thinking about your data gathering and the research methods you intend to use. Your interaction with the literature will continue throughout your research work, not just in order to set it up. In her research, Bruce (1994) noted that there were 'higher' purposes of a literature review, which she describes as a 'vehicle for learning'. As students' work progresses this purpose will become increasingly more prominent, whereby engaging with the literature actively influences the researcher. Bruce also noted that the review can serve as a 'research facilitator', whereby the literature considered comes to have an impact on the research project. Towards the end of your research you may be interested in drawing upon the literature to develop conceptual frameworks for analysis of data, and to consider why there are differences between your results and those in the literature and the explanations for these.

Some of the purposes identified above fit well with the experience of two Open University EdD students who were discussing in an online seminar how their literature reviews served different purposes at various stages of the research process. They considered the different ways in which their literature reviews evolved and the value of them at different points in their research:

I suppose, in very simple terms, the literature review provides a context for the research. At the start of the process, as we flounder in a sea of ideas for our research, searching, reading and thinking about the literature can help to inform the research focus and the question(s) and/or themes to be investigated. At the (even more uncomfortable?) stage of analysis, it provides a framework for comparison, and (perhaps) for explaining and understanding our empirical findings.

Firstly, understanding ideas from the literature does help to define your research question. I found that this definition was a lengthy and ongoing process, and I'm sure it's not finished yet. Appreciating how other people have understood 'your' topic adds depth to your own consideration of it and of course raises issues you might not have considered. Secondly, when you begin to collect data you can begin to look at what you've got in a more informed way. Some resonances with reading that you have carried out start to appear, and these build confidence in your own perceptions and conclusions.

(OU EdD Literature Review Seminar)

The literature review you undertake for your EdD will focus on important professional issues in education, and locate them within relevant academic traditions. This context is unique in doctoral research, and important in highlighting the distinctive nature of your work. Not only will your review need to contextualise the problem being researched, it will also need to underpin the implications you draw out for professional practice in education. You should aim to use the literature review to reflect on theory/practice issues, to connect explicitly with relevant policy initiatives, and to construct an argument about the educational relevance of your themes. Your literature review should exemplify how your thesis advances knowledge.

The character of different forms of literature

When an experienced research colleague, Martyn Hammersley, facilitated an online seminar for Open University EdD students focusing on 'Reviewing the Literature', a supervisor raised the important question of what counts as a literature review, what are its boundaries – should it be extended to people, and to professional literature? This question is particularly relevant for students engaged in a professional doctorate where issues related to their subject matter are discussed frequently in the media, professional journals and reports. Hammersley's response to this question is offered below:

It seems to me that one of the contrasts that define a literature review is with the data that are going to be used in the research. Literature, in the form of documents, and not just professional reports but even research texts, could form part of the data for a thesis. As such, they would be dealt with in the body of the thesis. What the literature review does, I suggest, is to set the context for the work that follows. In this respect, it may include professional as well as research literature; and of course that distinction is by no means clear-cut. At the same time, the differing character and reliability of items of literature need to be recognised. Some parts of the literature will serve as foundations, providing what is to be relied on as assumptions in your research, and in the case of these it is necessary to ensure that what is drawn on IS reliable. Other items will be used as suggestive models, and here what is important is their usefulness rather than their validity in their own right. Other sources may be used as negative models, as representing assumptions that are NOT to be made or models that are NOT to be followed. So there does need to be a flexible approach to dealing with different types of literature.

(OU EdD Literature Review Seminar)

It is important to think critically about what you actually select to read from all the references you retrieve. It is useful to ask yourself what contribution particular perspectives, concepts and findings may have for your research as you conduct your search. The quality of the information you obtain is likely to vary so you need to assess this when selecting material. This will inform your decision about whether it is worth spending more time on particular books, journal articles, Web pages, etc. Try to develop a checklist of necessary or important features to help you decide. You might consider some of the following:

- **Is the information properly referenced so that you can verify the points made?**

- **Does the author show awareness of developments in the field?**

- **Is it sufficiently up to date to be of value to your topic?**

- **Does the material fulfil what it led you to expect in the introduction or summary?**

- **If it is a research report, how valid is the methodology, and can you trust the results?**

- **Is there a bias – personal, political – that affects the way information is presented?**

- **If it is a discursive paper, does it give a balanced view of the topic?**

- **If it is a Web resource, is it clear who is responsible for it?**

- **If it has been cited, who by, and where?**

Do not be afraid to challenge assumptions and to discard any material that fails to meet your criteria.

Strategies for recording key points made in the literature

As you identify a range of articles and books that have a bearing on your study it is easy to feel overwhelmed by the volume of these and the time needed to read through them all. It is well worth looking out for reviews of work in the field you are working in and of overlapping fields. At first this may involve speed-reading to identify the focus of the article, and noting the main points made. At this stage you should pay particular attention to introductions, abstracts, headings and conclusions. As you do so, try to note down no more than two or three key points from each article; this should enable you to decide which ones are really important to follow up and which ones you can dismiss (anything that is outdated, for example). This is not to suggest that perspectives and concepts found in older literature, such as works by Bruner or Marx for example, should not be considered. You may find that the work of a classical theorist is still useful and relevant in relation to the research you have chosen to undertake. What you will need to do is to raise questions about the relevance of the literature for the area that you are focusing on.

You are likely to need to return to some of the articles that you have read at a later stage and reread material that appears to be especially relevant during the course of your research. It will be very important to develop an effective system for managing all the information that you accumulate. There is nothing more frustrating than not being able to locate a useful article or book because you failed to record references in a systematic way at the time you first located them.

Developing academic writing skills

Students often have difficulty in starting to write their reviews. There is a feeling that you have to collect everything first before you can write a review. Especially when using online searches, the searching process itself can become almost obsessive. It is actually much better to start writing immediately because writing needs to be viewed as a continuous process throughout your EdD, not a separate stage at the end. One way of getting started with your review is to consider the level and depth of knowledge needed as you focus on your core research question. Writing up the general subject area and the main issues of debate should be a relatively straightforward task. This does not require too much depth and is also something that many other researchers will have done. This literature can be acknowledged without attending to details or critical evaluations of each study. Again, this may involve speed-reading to identify the focus of the article and noting the main points made. At this stage you may find it helpful to find somebody else's general review in your subject area and examine it critically. A useful exercise is to work out how you might adapt this review to make it better suited to your own purposes. That can then form the basis for structuring your own general review.

Rudestam and Newton (1992) draw upon a metaphor of film-making in their discussion of doing a literature review. They note that in film-making there are 'long shots', 'medium shots' and 'close-ups'. For example, an EdD thesis researching how post-16 teaching impacts on what Initial Teacher Training (ITT) mentors do in their training role with student teachers deliberately divided the literature review into three themes, paralleling its three chapters of data analysis. The review began with a long shot, panning across the research territory, which revealed an absence of relevant literature on one key theme: how student teachers learn to teach post-16. The landscape was relatively empty, dotted with research on the post-16 curriculum and post-16 assessment in relation to policy debates, but lacking work on post-16 pedagogy. The long shot was important in establishing a justification for this theme, suggesting an original slant in an important policy area. It also allowed exploration of a wide range of texts to establish relevant background theory.

The medium shot took a closer look at research on mentoring and the mentor role. This established that there had been an explosion of interest in this aspect of teacher education over the last decade. The plethora of articles and books published could not possibly contribute equally to the argument emerging in the researcher's mind. The medium shot allowed comparison and contrast, and allowed the extraction of a number of lines of argument: for example, that mentoring is not as prescribed by policy-makers, but is idiosyncratic and context-dependent. It also showed no one model is yet dominant or generally accepted.

Zooming in for the close-up was the most detailed part of the review, but this could only be effective when the establishing shots had been completed. Research on challenge as a mentor strategy became critical. This enabled a theoretical perspective to emerge. It established a model or framework within which the research would be conducted, and it highlighted an appropriate methodology. It also complemented OFSTED data, suggesting a huge gap between academic or policy prescriptions about mentoring and mentoring practice in secondary schools. It revealed a level of detailed description and analysis which needed to inform the research. The close-up also allowed the researcher to return to the long shot, searching for something missed, or to reread what others had taken for granted or misinterpreted. Conducted in this way, the EdD literature review can allow research insights to be utilised in an original and professionally relevant way.

Critically examining an article

When engaging with the literature, Hart (2001) suggests that it is helpful to consider the following questions:

- **What are the key sources?**

- **What are the major issues and debates about the topic?**

- **What are the key theories, concepts and ideas?**

- **What are the main questions and problems that have been addressed?**

- **How is the knowledge structured and organised?**

- **How have approaches to these questions increased your knowledge and understanding?**

- **What are the political standpoints?**

Developing an argument

In your literature review you will be seeking to develop an argument that addresses particular research questions, drawing upon the ideas and observations of other researchers in your field whose work is relevant to your research. In your writing it is important that you do not simply describe a variety of perspectives, you need to engage with them and consider their implications for the issues you are concerned with or what the argument is going to be in relation to them. In doing so you are constructing an argument. One strategy that may help you do this effectively is to try to anticipate the questions a reader might ask in a critical examination of your review. The reader needs to understand clearly the points that you are making and the evidence to which you are referring in order to support your position. What you are attempting here is to develop a mutual understanding of your argument. Rudestam and Newton (1992) offer a helpful way of thinking about this.

> *A literature review ... [is] a coherent argument that leads to the description of a proposed study. There should be no mystery about the direction in which you are going ('Where are you going with this?' is a good question to ask yourself repeatedly in the review of the literature). You always need to state explicitly at the outset the goal of the paper and the structure of the evolving argument. By the end of the literature review, the reader should be able to conclude that, 'Yes, of course, this is the exact study that needs to be done at this time to move knowledge in this field a little further along.' The review attempts to convince the reader of the legitimacy of your assertions by providing sufficient logical and empirical support along the way.*

(Rudestam and Newton 1992: 47)

As you develop a deeper understanding of the area you are researching you simultaneously develop expertise in the field on which you are focusing. This expertise can be reflected in your writing style by the voice you adopt. If you too readily use quotations rather than your own voice you risk deferring authority to others. Quotations should be used selectively when they capture a point/concept in a way that is hard to reproduce, or where they offer strong support for a point you are making. The advantage of formulating your own words to describe particular concepts/theories is that it will deepen your grasp of these and serve to demonstrate your understanding of the complex material you are reviewing. You also need to avoid too frequently deferring to the authority of leading theorists in your field, for example by regularly starting sentences with phrases such as 'Vygotsky found ...' or 'Bruner argues ...', as this serves to shift the reader's attention away from the argument that you are constructing to the work of others.

What is needed is the adoption of a critical perspective when referring to the work of others. One way of doing this is to look at the themes that form the basis for your position and to draw upon their work to support the points that you are making. One key feature of a literature review is to attempt to impose order on these differences: to identify the main protagonists and how they relate to one another, and to show which research evidence contributes to which arguments and why. A further important part of the review process is the scrutiny of the research methodology employed and the form of analysis of the data collected. Do different positions on an issue derive from the nature of the evidence on which they are based and the ways in which that evidence was gathered? Are the conclusions justified on the basis of the evidence available? It is also important to bear in mind that you should not ignore or exclude references that contradict or question your case. It is essential that you try to be as objective possible, presenting both sides to any case and acknowledging where the weight of evidence falls.

The assessment of your literature review

The various assignments that you prepare during your EdD will provide you with valuable experience of the procedures and techniques involved, and of appropriate styles of writing, and contribute to the development of your thesis. You will also benefit from the advice and guidance offered by your supervisor that will help to refine your work.

Wallace and Poulson (2003) offer a helpful definition of a literature review by stating that it is a reviewer's critical account designed to convince a particular audience about what has been published about theory, research, practice or policy texts which indicate what is and is not known about one or more questions framed by the researcher. When you present your thesis for examination your examiners will be looking to see that the review embraces these elements and that the research student:

- **knows his or her subject and the key debates within the area of focus;**

- **is able to review and analyse the literature critically. You will need to provide a critical review of other work in the field; not just a list of relevant studies but a demonstration of your understanding of them. Think of this as providing a guided tour of a topic, pointing out important features (not every insignificant molehill);**

- is able to show that what the literature included clearly relates to the research questions being addressed, by showing that there is a clear rationale for the questions explored.

Conclusion

So far you have considered the contribution that the literature review can make to the development of your research plans and the coherence of the arguments you present in your thesis. You have also considered strategies for assessing the literature that you identify as relevant for your own investigation. Later you will consider the development of theoretical frameworks for the collection and analysis of your data. The literature that you include in your study will contribute to this process.

4 Ethics: Issues, Dilemmas and Problems

All research has ethical dimensions. In qualitative research, and particularly case studies that feature aspects of social life, ethical issues are inescapable. In quantitative research, the link between statistics and ethics may at first appear to be tenuous but, as Sammons (1989) has argued, the phrase 'rules of conduct', which governs the uses of statistical work, is the key to their connection. To investigate ethics for the educational researcher we explore some of the issues, dilemmas and problems that doctorate in education students have faced in the conduct of their research.

This chapter covers:

- **ethical issues in research;**

- **ethical issues at the research design stage;**

- **privacy, confidentiality and anonymity;**

- **gaining access;**

- **research relationships;**

- **collaboration;**

- **writing up and reporting findings;**

- **dissemination of data.**

Why is an understanding of ethical issues important for you as a student on a doctorate in education programme? A doctorate in education is a major piece of work and needs to be taken very seriously. This is particularly important as the product of your research is going to be a thesis that will be available to the public as well as other researchers in a library. You will need to show that you have followed ethical guidelines in the conduct of your research and taken account of the due moral and legal implications linked to your research activities. Clarity in terms of how you have designed your research, collected and analysed the data, and written it up, is essential if you are to demonstrate ethical responsibility. Understanding some of the ethical issues involved in achieving transparency in your research, therefore, is a good place to start.

Ethical issues in research

Ethical issues will most likely be highly specific to your particular research project. They will depend on whether you are conducting interviews and surveys, or using other methodologies such as participant observation or action research. Some of these issues may be concerned with confidentiality, identification, freedom to publish, and the nature of professional standards. Burgess (1989) discusses how such issues can arise in dramatic circumstances in educational research and particularly in the day-to-day experience of conducting research in schools. He raises a number of questions in his reflections on ethical problems (1989: 2):

- **What should individuals be told about the conduct of social research?**

- **Is secret research justifiable?**

- **Is secret research desirable?**

- **What data can be collected 'openly'?**

- **How should data be disseminated?**

- **What protection can be given to those individuals who participate in social and educational research?**

   As you plan your research you will find that all the above questions are relevant to a greater or lesser extent to what you wish to do. Bryman (2001), in his discussion of ethical principles, identifies four main areas: whether there is harm to the participants; whether there is lack of informed consent; whether there is an invasion of privacy; and whether deception is involved. As we consider the different stages of research and what ethical considerations you will need to take into account, you should remind yourself where Bryman's four main areas of ethical principles emerge.

Ethical issues at the research design stage

Ethical considerations come into every aspect of your research and begin when you first plan your initial proposal and indicate a choice of research methods. Bassey (1999) argues that there are three major ethical values: respect for democracy; respect for truth; and respect for persons. He suggests that in a democratic society, researchers should have the freedom to investigate and ask questions, to give and receive information, to be able to express ideas and criticise those of others and have the freedom to publish their research findings. Of course, having the freedom to conduct research in this way imposes responsibilities of respect for truth in terms of data collection, data analysis and the reporting of findings. It also imposes responsibilities of respect for persons so that the respondents' ownership of the data is acknowledged and both dignity and privacy are preserved. As guiding principles, the three major ethical values described by Bassey are highly honourable, but do they assume that a society that is democratic both regards truth and respects persons at all times? It could be argued that to one degree or another we are always researching in societies that do not match these requirements and, therefore, we should consider the implications of that. Should researchers modify what they count as ethical accordingly? Or should we accept that to one degree or another, in order to carry out research, researchers must expect to be unethical? Speaking of the roles an ethnographer engages in, Ball (1993) says of researchers:

> *They must charm the respondents into co-operation. They must learn to blend in or pass in the research setting, put up with the boredom and the horrors of the empty notebook, cringe in the face of faux pas made in front of those whose co-operation they need, and engage in the small deceptions and solve the various ethical dilemmas which crop up in most ethnographies.*

(Ball 1993: 32)

It is not, therefore, as straightforward as it might at first appear to take an ethical stance in all aspects of your research. What issues should be considered in the early stages of research design and proposal writing?

Having a sound rationale for why you want to carry out your particular research project is important, and for students on a doctorate in education programme this is often linked to their professional workplace or setting. In your design you will need to consider how you will collect data that will produce or enhance knowledge and how your choice of research approach will produce a certain kind of knowledge. EdD students have also to consider how their professional knowledge impacts upon their research design and data collection. One EdD student who researched the vocational dental practitioner (VDP) explained the issue as follows:

> *There are many ways in which I could undertake my research to gain an insight into the experiences of the VDPs and their trainers. However, a collaborative enquiry approach, where I spend time with my participants as VT [vocational training] progresses, will provide a richer source of data than a more conventional large-scale survey could offer. To achieve this I must go into the VT practices and interview my participants. But I must keep in contact with them throughout the 12 months of VT; a one-off interview will not suffice. I must capture the VT experience and my data gathering and analysis will revolve around this quest. Anything less than a truly interpretative approach will not be appropriate; it will not provide the nature or quality of data essential to this study.*

(Cabot 2004: 50–1)

Why is the above an ethical issue? In designing his research project the student recognised that the knowledge he wished to access could only be gained in a particular way and through repeatedly returning to the participants across the course of one year. The nature, validity and quality of the data depended upon a particular approach in the design of the research. The professional knowledge of the researcher was also an ethical consideration at the design stage:

> *Every participant must have confidence in me as a researcher; a researcher who genuinely wants to move vocational education forward in a positive and appropriate way. There can be nothing covert about this research. What my background says about me shouts louder than anything I can say.*

(Cabot 2004: 53)

Transparency and openness in the design of this research project was essential if the student was to research the dental vocational training experience successfully. It had to be set up in a way that would allow the respondents to trust the researcher so that rich, valuable data could be collected. Who the researcher is may also have an impact upon the collection of data and in this highly professional context where the researcher had 'insider' knowledge it would not have been possible to be anything other than overt. However, from whom data are collected can raise a number of issues about confidentiality and anonymity, as we will now consider.

Privacy, confidentiality and anonymity

Educational researchers, it has been argued (Bassey 1999), have a moral duty to respect the privacy and dignity of those whom they research. This moral duty of the researcher extends to all participants and every spectrum of society, whether they are institutional colleagues or young children in playgroups or schools. It can be particularly difficult in small organisations or schools to maintain the anonymity of respondents, particularly from each other! How data are collected about some respondents can also bring an ethical dilemma. For example, how do you balance the privacy of individuals against the right of the trustworthy researcher to publish, or the privacy of interview respondents when the interviewer possesses evidence of which they are not aware?

Just such an issue arose for one EdD student who discussed her dilemma in the electronic conferencing environment:

> *The site of my research is the company where my husband is employed. I currently have an interesting ethical problem in that he has given me a crucial piece of information concerning previous learning opportunities in the company but he believes that no one will tell me about them in my interviews because of the circumstances prevailing at the time (it is a complicated story!). Ethically, I have not obtained this knowledge during the course of my fieldwork, but if I ignore it, I risk cutting myself off from some important information.*

The seminar moderator replies:

Yes, you may have to forgo the use of certain pieces of evidence if it is possible to identify or predict that it will harm the participant in any way. In a sense this bald statement should be qualified by the statement 'as far as you can'. This is the ethical injunction. However, there is a more pragmatic concern, which is that it may damage future relations preventing you collecting data from those people. However, it may be possible to negotiate release of the data and you may be able to protect people's interests by anonymising the data. The problem you have refers to the difficulty of balancing the demands of different ethical precepts which may at times conflict. So validity may be aspiration but this may conflict with the need to protect informants.

(OU EdD Ethics Seminar)

As can be seen from the above conversation, conducting your research in an ethical manner is not simply a matter of adhering to a set of rules. It requires a great deal of thought at every stage of your thesis. Ethical issues are intertwined with knowledge through the values individuals hold and the processes of research. The British Educational Research Association guidelines for ethical research (BERA 1992) add a fourth principle to the three discussed by Bassey (1999). BERA guidelines state that researchers should have respect for educational research itself. By this they mean that researchers should not conduct their research in ways that will damage the future enquiries of other researchers. As you plan, research, analyse and write up your data you should try to keep all these ethical principles in mind. To help you to do this we have identified a few key issues in the processes of research.

Gaining access

All codes of ethics such as the BERA guidelines (see BERA 1992) place the principle of informed consent at the centre of ethical research activity. However, problems can still arise even when consent has been obtained. Often when a qualitative study is set up it is not possible to specify initially exactly what data will be collected or how it will be used. It could be argued, therefore, that individuals are not fully informed. Burgess (1989) reports how he gained agreement to sit in on job interviews for teachers in schools on the basis that he would be introduced to all the candidates by the headteacher or he would introduce himself. However, this rarely happened in a systematic way and, given the power relations involved in the situation, it was not surprising that none of the candidates objected even though they were given the opportunity to do so. How far should informed consent be taken in order to sustain the concept of respect for persons?

In quantitative research the issue of informed consent is equally pertinent. Where statistical enquiries involve professionals working in an institution such as a hospital or school, it is important that respondents understand that their participation is voluntary. As the researcher you should offer them the right to refuse for whatever reason should they wish to do so. This, of course, can be difficult for you as a researcher, especially if your sample is not very large and you do not receive many returns to your enquiry. Other statistical data that you may wish to use may be publicly available information and here the ethical concepts of respect for truth and democracy will need to be considered in the way that you use this data.

Research relationships

Relationships between the researcher and the researched have been discussed by a number of researchers (Riddell 1989; Simons 1989). Often, ethical discussions concerning research relationships are based around covert versus overt research and the merits and demerits of each. Where researchers take on a participant observer role it is sometimes done covertly to protect the validity of the data. For example, Hockey (1986) researched a group of young squaddies on the streets of Belfast, in training camps and doing exercises in the Canadian wastelands. He had gained access by seeking permission from the commanding officer of the battalion. As he had been a soldier himself he was able to deceive those whom he researched about his identity as a researcher for the sake of authenticity. Such research raises the question, how far is covert research justified? What is to be gained that cannot be obtained through overt research? Burgess (1989) argues that ethical issues concerning research relationships are not confined to the use of participant observation and 'open' or 'closed' research. He suggests that questions of access, power, harm, deception, secrecy and confidentiality are all issues that have to be considered and resolved in the research context.

When your research project involves interviewing, there are several ethical issues that need consideration. Interviews are usually dialogues between two people, both of whom bring their own social background and personality to the situation. You must therefore decide on your intended relationship with the informant. Le Voi (2000) argues that qualitative work necessarily entails involvement; it cannot be done in an 'objective', neutral and/or disengaged manner if it is to yield any worthwhile insight into the informant's world. This issue is discussed by EdD students researching within their own institutions. One student commented:

I was known to all the participants in the interviews with mentors, by virtue of my role within the HEI. While this may have meant that I did not need to establish rapport in the same way that would have been necessary had we been strangers to each other, it may have had other effects upon the interviews, in terms of the 'sincerity' of participants' responses ... In selecting a semi-structured approach in order to gain some consistency in the subject matter explored within the interviews I needed to be extremely alert to the effect that this choice has upon the interviewees, particularly in view of my role in the HEI–school partnership.

(Wilson 2004: 81)

Le Voi (2000) goes on to suggest that in most interview research the question of 'ownership' is quite clear: the research is planned and initiated by the researcher, and therefore he or she 'owns the rights' to the data and the conclusions drawn from them. However, this can make for an uneasy relationship, and often a sense of guilt, because you are not genuinely participating in the relationship but rather using the informant as a source. In these situations there is no intent to continue the relationship after the research is finished. Under some circumstances the participants may benefit from this kind of distant research relationship. Some informants may welcome the chance to talk freely to a stranger and to work out their own attitudes to what is happening. A similar dilemma is also present when researching inside your own professional setting and is described in the following way by an EdD student:

> *My role during the investigation involved ambiguities that I assume also affect others undertaking prac-*
> *titioner research in institutions in which they work. There were some advantages to my position. As a*
> *college 'insider' I had some understanding of the course arrangements and events I was witnessing;*
> *however, I had never taught on the course in question and had a degree of distance from it that helped to*
> *increase my objectivity about what I saw. The personal and social relationships involved in conducting*
> *the study needed sensitive handling. To tutor respondents I was a colleague and in one case a personal*
> *friend, and I was aware of a degree of instrumentalism in my 'use' of them for my own goals. My con-*
> *cerns were defused when these turned out to be congruous with respondents' own aims to promote articu-*
> *lation of graphic design as a field; it also explained the enthusiasm of tutors to support the study, which*
> *I had found surprising at first. At the beginning of the study, students saw me in discussion with their*
> *tutors and concluded I was a member of staff. When I explained I was undertaking research towards a*
> *qualification, there was a noticeable shift in their attitudes, and it appeared I took on a quasi-student*
> *persona that led them to feel less restrained when I was present.*

(Logan 2005: 64–5)

Both the EdD students quoted above faced issues linked to being an insider researcher. As insiders they possessed intimate knowledge of the community and its members. Being an insider can create some difficulties such as being too familiar, taking things for granted, displaying bias towards the informants and finding it hard to ask questions about shared events and experiences. There are, though, a number of advantages, including ease of access and greater rapport with participants, and setting up the research is less time-consuming and therefore cheaper to carry out.

Researching in your own work environment can be problematic where research is conducted among friends or neighbours. This is because the degree of disclosure entailed by the research changes the nature of the relationships. In some contexts certain participants become what is known as 'key informants' because of their relevance to the research being conducted or because their position within the institution means they are able to access highly valuable research data.

When conducting an ethnographic study you may place considerable reliance upon your key informants, especially as they become more important to your research as data collection progresses. Bryman (2001) argues that while key informants can be of great help to an ethnographer, and provide support during the stress of fieldwork, there are risks attached. The researcher may come to rely unduly upon the key informant rather than seeing the social reality through the eyes of other members of the setting. Incidents that occur may be perceived to have a particular interpretation by the key informant and this may not be shared by other respondents.

Incidents that happen during the collection of data can assist you, as the researcher, as they accentuate the features of the social reality you are investigating. Such instances are known as 'critical incidents'. Critical phases and incidents in teachers' careers have been explored by Sikes et al. (1985), a classic study, which has much relevance for educational researchers today. The term 'critical incident' has also been used widely in the research literature on classroom teachers. Such incidents are often synonymous with times of strain such as the beginnings and endings of teachers' careers, or turning points brought about by surprise or shock. The authors identify three types of critical phase: extrinsic, intrinsic and personal. The initial critical incident is usually followed by a counter incident which is then successfully managed. The counter incident does not introduce new ideas but acts to crystallise ideas, attitudes and beliefs that are already being formed. The interpretation of critical and counter incidents during the collection of data may be assisted by taking a collaborative approach.

Collaboration

Establishing a working relationship in order to engage in collaborative research is an alternative approach that can help you to understand the data you have collected. However, this is not unproblematic and researchers will need to consider the implications of engaging in collaborative research given the power relationships involved in terms of access to knowledge. Le Voi (2000) explores the notion of collaboration, and suggests that some loosening of the power relationship between researcher and informants could be valuable. It may be possible, for instance, to show your report to the informants and obtain their comments on it, or to run a group session to discuss your conclusions.

The important thing here, however, is that you do not promise what you cannot deliver. There should be some kind of 'contract' between researcher and informants – not necessarily a written document, but at least a series of implicit and/or explicit agreements by which you, the researcher, and your informants are bound. You will need to promise your informants anonymity, for example – that what they say to you will not be used in a way which enables them to be identified – and you must keep that promise even if it is professionally inconvenient to do so. (Alternatively, if your research leads you to finding out things about people over whom you have some control or power of decision, you must make your position clear to them.) If you have no power to remedy any 'wrongs' reported to you, this must also be made clear. The location of your research, in an industrial or educational setting, may also have an impact upon what is expected from you as a researcher, as explained by Cheri Logan:

Questions of trust were highlighted in regard to industry respondents, especially managers, who were more concerned for the confidentiality of their operations. The statements about my purpose, research standards and ethics that I made to all participants were crucial in securing cooperation from practitioner respondents, whereas those in college seemed to listen politely until I had finished, but not be particularly interested. The response encountered from commercial contexts made me develop and maintain higher standards in regard to confidentiality, potential conflicts of interest and use of data than I might have if restricted to the educational environment. It made me a better, more reliable researcher as a result, and enabled me to develop skills in undertaking research in non-educational settings that are of potential use for future inquiry.

(Logan 2005: 65)

You will, therefore, need to be alert to the levels of confidence required in different research contexts and make sure that you can protect each of your respondents through both assuring anonymity and using data in a responsible way so that no harm is caused to them. Any element of collaboration must also be an explicit item of the contract, and you must make sure you will be able to deliver what you promise. Will there be *time* for collaboration, for example – will your report be written in time for a group meeting or for informants to read it? To what extent will such feedback interact with any promise of anonymity you wish to make? And what do you propose to *do* about the outcome of the feedback process? If the informants do not agree with what you have written, are you bound to change it? Or do you undertake to represent their views as well as your own, giving them 'right of reply'? Or will you just take note of their reactions and use them if appropriate, retaining control in your own hands? These are all decisions that only you can make in the context of your research setting.

Writing up and reporting findings

Since your thesis will be public, it is particularly important that the rights of sources are respected where necessary. If you are obtaining information *about* individuals, it is clearly important that privacy is respected. If you are obtaining information *through* individuals (as informants), you may need to take steps to preserve anonymity, as journalists try to do.

There may be occasions during interviews where respondents will tell you things that are 'just between ourselves' while the tape recorder is still on. The dilemma here for the researcher is how to use this 'confidential' information, if at all. Sometimes it is possible to gain understandings of situations in this way that can then be utilised in other interviews without breaking confidentiality.

If you obtain private information, you must be sure to maintain confidentiality, both in the writing up of your research thesis and in your research records. You may have to keep records under lock and key. Remember, there is a substantial understanding of trust between you and your sources, and ultimately your own academic integrity, perhaps also that of your profession, needs to sustain that trust through conducting your research appropriately.

Throughout the research process you need to take a reflexive stance so that you consider the implications of your methods, values, biases and decisions for the knowledge about the social world you generate. As you collect, analyse and write up your data you should be aware of and acknowledge the role of yourself as the researcher in the construction of knowledge. The stance that you take as you write up your data implicates you in the construction of knowledge represented in your thesis and reflects the choices that you have made throughout the research process. The importance of taking such a stance is revealed by a male EdD student who was researching gender issues in design and technology in a primary school:

Through my reflection on the interviews and the classroom observations I sought to understand the boys' constructions of what it is to be male and the girls' constructions of what it is to be female because it is how people construct these narratives in particular ways that makes gender real. Had I started off with a clear theoretical perspective and a clear understanding of and commitment to a post-structuralist approach to this study, I would have had these thoughts in the forefront of my mind as I planned the study and conducted the interviews and classroom observations and I am sure that I would have done some things differently.

(Hamlin 2004: 52)

Such reflection is an important ethical consideration in all research but for John Hamlin, who conducted feminist research, principles of informed consent meant that:

Individuals have the freedom to define themselves and their situations in their own terms, unconstrained by the demands, standards and agendas of others.

(Hamlin 2004: 54)

This student's research involved working with young children and issues surrounding informed consent were complex to resolve. Responsibility for informed consent is clearly implicated in the earliest decisions that a researcher takes about the subject, design and context of the research.

Dissemination of data

Dissemination of data begins well before the final presentation of your thesis or the first published article after gaining your doctorate. If you have decided upon a collaborative approach when collecting your data, you will be required to feed back to your informants well before your final draft. There may be a number of reasons why informants would like access to your data before they are finalised in written form. If you are researching in a school, for example, senior members of staff will occasionally attempt to gain access to research data to inform future policy decisions (Burgess 1988). Also occasionally, informants become worried about what they have said and wish to have 'their tape' returned or to change what was originally said. Such activities can be an important and valuable part of the collaborative research process where informants listen to or read a transcript of what was said and, based on reflection, amend or agree their original comments. Collaboration, therefore, can provide a second interpretation of the data which may provide additional validation thus confirming the findings of the research.

If you intend to publish sections of your thesis in article format for a journal you will need to consider the rights of your informants over the data you intend to use. It can be very difficult to draw the line between ethical and unethical practices in your research. Collecting 'honest' data sometimes involves not telling participants everything about your research. Selecting a portion of your research to report in a journal has similar complications as you cannot include everything that you put in your thesis to explain your research story. There are often no 'right' answers to ethical dilemmas and problems and what you finally include in your thesis and published work drawn from your thesis will need to reflect the ethical principles on which you founded your research.

Conclusion

This chapter has explored some of the ethical issues, dilemmas and problems that can arise in the conduct of educational research, and the responsibilities of the educational researcher. Today, ethical issues cover both moral and legal dilemmas in the conduct of research. As a researcher you will have to balance responsibilities to those who are the subject of the research against presenting the findings in an uncompromising way to a wider audience. Ethical problems begin with the choice of research method. Once the research is under way issues of honesty in research relationships can become problematic, particularly if the focus of the research is not yet clear. Many EdD students conduct insider research and issues of power relations as well as those of personal bias caused by familiarity will have to be resolved. Publication and dissemination of research is an ethical responsibility that all those who enter into research have to consider alongside what might be the benefit for the research participants.

Very often, a consideration of ethics is left until the end of texts about doing research. We have deliberately placed this chapter on ethics early in the book as we hope you will consider the ethical issues and dilemmas that may emerge at each stage of your research, beginning with developing a theoretical framework, which is outlined in the next chapter. It is through a consideration of ethical problems and dilemmas in the processes of conducting research that you will extend your professional knowledge as an educator and develop reflexive practice.

5 Developing Theoretical Frameworks

By now you will have developed ideas about the research questions or issues you want to address or solve and will have undertaken some reading around your chosen topic. However, a research process cannot be seen as linear and straightforward, as in the way this book is set out for example, in a seemingly logical sequence. Instead, doing research is akin to completing a jigsaw puzzle with lots of different pieces which only make sense as a whole when they eventually come together. Researching, as you will be aware, is a highly complex process that requires constant reflection, amendment, adjustment and refinement if it is to succeed.

This chapter, therefore, aims to help you complete parts of your puzzle by looking at theories you will have to consider when thinking about how you want to develop research. This means being concerned with:

(a) a theoretical subject-based dimension in relation to your chosen topic, the literature and the research questions you ask;

(b) methodologies, that is theories which underpin the research methods you would like to employ;

(c) how the relationship between both sets of theories relate to your overall research design.

The following two chapters are, therefore, mainly about 'theories'. This chapter will deal with theories to be considered when developing your conceptual framework and Chapter 6 concerns theories you need to think about in relation to research methods you want to employ. The aim is twofold: on the one hand, such discussions should help you to gain a better understanding about issues relevant to educational research in general, and on the other, they should help you to think more specifically about theoretical issues in relation to your own research. As you will have gathered, almost every aspect of research at this level is embedded in an abundance of theories. One of the difficulties you, as a researcher face, is to disentangle the numerous theoretical points of view you come across and make sense of these for your own research. To start you on this process of thinking about theories the chapter addresses the following issues:

- **thinking about theories;**

- **linking theory and practice to research;**

- **developing theory out of data;**

- **developing a conceptual framework.**

Thinking about theories

Many students at the beginning of their doctoral research have clear strategies and goals in mind. They start the doctoral programme with ideas about what to read, which theoretical framework to develop, which research methods to use and how to go about collecting and analysing specific sets of data. Other students are less certain in these early stages. They have an understanding of what it is they want to investigate but every step they take seems laden with yet more complexities and with no apparent outcomes in sight. Doing educational research can be likened to planning a journey where the destination is apparently predetermined but there are several pathways of getting there, each with its own particular attractions and potential pitfalls. One of the many stumbling blocks, though potentially exciting, is the abundance of theoretical perspectives a researcher faces. But why do we need to refer to theories at all? Mercer (1991: 42) offers the following explanation: 'One function of theories is to set the agendas for research – to generate certain kinds of questions which the research will attempt to answer. Another function is to provide a "universe of discourse" within which the discussion and explanation of research findings can take place.' Such a universe of discourse is about sharing ideas and practices within particular research communities. The research community will include not only your supervisor and fellow researchers but also academics and professionals in your area of education who have an interest in your research and need to understand the arguments and findings you present.

The next question to ask is, 'Where does theory come from?' Predictably, there are many different answers. Theory, on the one hand, comes from your own professional practice, from academics and fellow researchers whose literature you have read. However, doing academic research is also about expanding either existing theoretical perspectives or building new theories out of the data gathered, or indeed both. Such theory-building can involve developing subject-based constructs or a new combination of research methods. Think of it as completing the puzzle. There are no fixed points to begin the building process. In the end, however, sharing research findings with others will add to the appreciation of that picture and stimulate further theory development.

Professional knowledge

In the context of the professional doctorate, theory, it could be argued, is meaningless without context and practical application. As a professional educator you have developed your own theories (see Schön 1987) and gained a great deal of knowledge and understanding about your area of work and other aspects of your personal life.

Concepts of knowledge and understanding are problematic. Most teachers have several types of knowledge which constantly change, sometimes in very subtle ways of which they are not always aware. As professionals, they are expected to have a sound knowledge of their teaching subjects (or discipline knowledge, Scott et al. 2004) and to appreciate how that understanding shapes their approaches to learning and teaching. Knowledge, therefore, can relate to what you as a professional know about your subject of teaching, the *knowing that*, or to teacher knowledge (Calderhead 1987), that is, knowledge that experienced teachers have gained about how to best engender students' learning, the *knowing how*. In the context of doing a professional doctorate you will be concerned with both your subject knowledge and your teacher knowledge. Both relate to the practice of teaching or to your professional context as an educator/teacher/staff developer concerned with learning and teaching. Consider the following statement:

> In the teaching profession itself it seems rare for teachers to generally consider what they know about teaching in ways that might be documented and portrayed through text. Rather, their understanding – hence the professional knowledge base – continues to be dominated by the sharing of teaching experiences, critical incidents, and specific incidents, within which knowledge of practice is implicitly embedded. Therefore, it seems reasonable to assert that more often than not it is up to the individual teachers to draw their own conclusions about a particular instance from another's telling of that incident, rather than to have supplied some form of knowledge claim that is supported by generalisable statements based on reproducible events and experiences.

(Loughran et al. 2003: 868)

Loughran and his colleagues argue that one of the difficulties associated with documenting teacher knowledge is that it is closely associated with seeing knowledge in practice. Practice is regarded as something related to skills, something one can do provided there is enough exercise. In terms of research, therefore, research questions arise out of practice or everyday reality within a professional context and feed back into practice once conclusions have been drawn. Individual teacher knowledge can thus be the source and inspiration that leads to further thinking about issues that have arisen in the practical context. It is possible that this thinking about issues or events that have occurred or are occurring in your everyday practice has led you to want to undertake in-depth research at doctoral level. It is likely that you will have done a fair amount of reading around your chosen topic, even before you have submitted your application. Let us assume, therefore, that you have been able to discover in your reading a wide range of different perspectives, arguments, theorising and pieces of research undertaken by scholars and practitioners in your area. Consider the following points raised by a first-year EdD student we have called 'Mary':

> *I am a Nurse Teacher working in a new university and like most (if not all) of you I am keen to do a good job. I have been a teacher for almost 20 years and over that time the curriculum delivered has gone through many changes. The product (qualified nurse), however, it could be argued, has stayed very much the same. My observations over the years have led me to question what makes a good nurse.*
>
> *My question therefore looks at different types of curricula and asks whether there is a qualitative difference in the product. I thought at the outset that my question was very straightforward. However, here we are three weeks in and I already want to change the focus of the second part of the study. My early reading has turned up facts that I had not anticipated and I am now beginning to think that what I had articulated for years 2 and 3 was a little naive. I am almost afraid to pick up a book or read another article in case I change my mind again.*

(EdD Seminar 2002)

As you can see, reading a lot can be quite confusing to begin with. Mary brings to the research her own professional knowledge and experience, only to find that she has to cope with an increasing number of uncertainties, particularly at the early stages of her doctorate. Most research students experience problems at this point. They know that they are expected to consider theories and develop their own construct, yet are not quite sure where to start. Consider the following statement made by another relatively new research student working towards a professional doctorate in education:

> *Carrying out a critical review of the literature causes me considerable difficulties. For example, I think that the term 'critical' has pejorative overtones. Applied to carrying out a literature review it implies that the work of others is flawed or lacking in some way or other. Furthermore, how can a novice researcher like myself possibly have the gall to criticise a published researcher or a paper or article that has appeared in a peer reviewed academic journal?*

(Email from EdD Student 2004)

This research student was in the process of outlining his theoretical framework for his research. However, he had read almost too much and found it increasingly difficult to cope with a range of disparate theories and with the requirement to look at these critically. It would not be surprising if you, too, felt that you have entered a theoretical minefield where it is difficult to see paths and directions to pursue. Furthermore, you may think that all you have known before no longer seems as relevant or as important as you once thought. Foucault (1972: 21) puts it aptly when he says, 'there is negative work to be carried out first: we must rid ourselves of a whole mass of notions, each of which, in its own way, diversifies the theme of continuity.' In other words, we have to undo, at least to some extent, previous suppositions and allow ourselves to be challenged with new and different perspectives which may or may not be relevant to the research questions in mind. It may be a confusing but necessary process in the early stages of research. The next step is to relate some but not all theoretical perspectives and research findings to your research question(s), to clarify and map concepts you want to employ as well as to construct your own theoretical framework. This is an ongoing process – one that demands constant rethinking, adjusting and eventual fine-tuning, and right from its early stages of perception to the very end of writing up your thesis.

Linking theory and practice to research

When thinking about your own professional context together with your areas of knowl-edge and understanding, you will see that, in your own mind at least, there is some kind of connection or harmony between context, theory and practice. Your research interest will have developed out of your professional practice. The process of reflection will have helped you to make sense, to develop theory, out of what you know and believe in. However, how do you know that your own thoughts about theories and practices are appropriate to the wider professional field, let alone to the research community interested in the outcome of your doctoral studies? Furthermore, what is the relationship between theory and practice? To what extent do theory, practice and research depend on each other? Predictably, there are no straightforward answers to these questions. To begin with, it is not easy to settle on a definition of the term 'theory', although a research thesis may be failed for what may be seen as inadequate theory development! Theory as a concept is often used in conjunction with interpretation and the construction of meaning to express the way we think about issues and the contribution it makes to educational matters. The pursuit of theory in educational research is considered to be essentially worthwhile, even necessary. All new insights, no matter how small, therefore make a valid contribution to the larger field of educational theory. If theory is about 'thinking', then practice, it can be argued, is concerned with 'doing', and in terms of research, with methods and procedures. However, behind the 'doing' aspect there are philosophical issues and personal belief systems. Even if these are not explicitly stated, they help researchers to understand connections and to frame their research design and evaluation so that the final outcome can be accepted and shared by the wider professional community.

Usher and Bryant (1989) provide a useful way of understanding the complex rela-tionship between theory, practice and research by referring to a 'captive triangle'. The metaphor they use depicts the way in which these three elements of the triangle are conventionally used in relation to each other. However, the word 'captive', they argue, points to a restricted understanding of the triangular relationship.

> *The idea of the 'triangle' represents what we wish to subject to critical and demystifying scrutiny, namely that theory and research are a foundation, or base, with practice as a superstructure or apex. This foun-dationalism implies that the relationship of theory and research to practice is always one where the for-mer are applied to the latter. We are, therefore 'captive' to application and ultimately foundationalism and we can only free ourselves from this if we first recognise the nature of our captivity.*

(Usher and Bryant 1989: 4)

Such conventional understanding of the relationship between theory, research and practice, Usher and Bryant argue, is often misleading and inappropriate. It promises 'good practice' by getting theory right and doing the right kind of research. However, the authors argue that such a triangle needs to be opened up, although it can never be dispensed with entirely. We can never be sure that anyone of these three elements is more important than the other two. It therefore means acknowledging the situatedness of the research and being prepared to engage in dialogue with ourselves and others and with different kinds of knowledge for the sake of critical and reflective practice.

Thus we can begin to recognise that there is a relationship between theory, research and practice and that this relationship is constantly changing as the research progresses and the researcher's knowledge and understanding develops. The point for you to bear in mind is that there are no predetermined ways of dealing with either theory or practice. Much depends on the kind of questions you ask and methodological approaches you want to develop.

Furthermore, a distinction can be made between *normative* and *factual* conceptions of 'theory'. Normative theory – which is often implicit in the 'captive triangle' – refers to abstract principles that guide action, indicating what should and should not be done in particular circumstances and why. The more factual conception is linked to the acknowledgement of *how things are* rather than how they should be. A further sense of theory, which is the essence of 'critical theory', brings these two conceptions together. In critical theory, it is believed to be possible to infer *what ought to be done* directly out of an understanding of what is observable in practice (The Open University 2001).

Developing shared understanding about theories used in research is therefore an integral part of reaching agreement among those who make their research findings available to others engaged in similar academic or professional areas. As a doctoral research student, for example, you need to ensure that those who supervise you together with those who will eventually read your final thesis share an understanding of key theories and concepts you have used. It is important that they follow your line of argument, understand the way you have looked at and developed your theoretical framework and analysed your data. Thereafter, however, if your findings are to be meaningful, your aim must be to share these with colleagues in your professional field with similar interests and concerns. Thus the tension perceived in the 'captive' triangle is eased and allowed to flow into other spheres of academic knowledge and professional practice.

Developing theory out of data

Let us assume that you are interested in finding out the relevance of e-learning to students on an MA programme in the health service. There are two ways of developing your research design: it can be deductive or inductive. The deductive approach would suggest that you adopt prevalent theories used in the context of e-learning by doing the appropriate literature review. In other words, what is involved in hypothetico-deductive method is the logical derivation of hypotheses from a theory that are then to be subjected to test. You would then devise a questionnaire to be sent to students, to be followed with interviews of the MA course team. The inductive approach, however, would start with the data gathering, and on the basis of data analysis you would develop your own theoretical models in conjunction with available literature on that topic. Such an inductive approach is particularly useful where the literature around your chosen research question is relatively underdeveloped.

Both the 'inductivist' and the 'deductivist' models correspond to styles of doing research; both have philosophical flaws which enable them to be criticised. In practice, most research projects involve both models to some extent. However, as Wengraf (2001) argues, each model must correspond to some real experience of the researcher. In his view, both are appropriate as descriptions of what researchers experience as happening at different moments of the research cycle and that another relationship between the inductivist and the deductivist models may be that of level. In other words, researchers can use both at different times of research.

Grounded theory

The inductivist 'grounded theory approach', however, remains a popular one with many research students. Grounded theory is a mode of qualitative analysis that seems to appeal to the imagination although when Glaser and Strauss introduced it they did not present grounded theorising as only appropriate to qualitative research, a chapter of their book applied it also to quantitative work. However, if done properly, it is, like all other approaches, very demanding.

A grounded theory is one that is inductively derived from the phenomenon it represents. That is, it is discovered, developed, and provisionally verified through systematic data collection and analysis of data pertaining to that phenomenon. Therefore, data collection, analysis, and theory stand in reciprocal relationship with each other. One does not begin with theory and then prove it. Rather, one begins with an area of study and what is then relevant to that area of study is allowed to emerge.

(Strauss and Corbin 1990: 23)

The grounded theory approach therefore is a qualitative research method that emerged as an alternative strategy to more traditional approaches to scientific enquiry. Glaser and Strauss's first book, *The Discovery of Grounded Theory*, was published in 1967. Both Glaser (1978) and Strauss (1987), and thereafter Strauss and Corbin (1990), have developed the approach in somewhat different ways. However, the term 'grounded theory' implies the application of a systematic set of procedures for the gathering and analysing of data out of which theory is developed. Strauss and Corbin (1990) advise that grounded theory procedures have to be practised through continued research so that one can gain sufficient understanding about how grounded theory works. There is interplay between data collection, data analysis conceptualisation/theorising and constant comparison which is central to grounded theory. Nevertheless, many researchers adopt a 'partial' grounded theory approach in which data is collected and then theorised upon without paying attention to the formal implementation of grounded theory procedures. Strauss and Corbin (1990) plead for *theoretical sensitivity* which, in their view, refers to the personal qualities of the researcher. Theoretical sensitivity can indicate that the researcher is aware of the subtleties of meaning of data and the understanding researchers bring to the research situation. However, such sensitivity is reflected in the questioning of the research process itself and the researcher's learning that has taken place because of it. Reflexivity therefore does not only refer to the development of new theories but also to the reflective process the individual researcher attaches to its outcome. Horton Merz (2002), in her research, refers to 'the journey through an emergent design and its path for understanding'. She argues that researchers should go beyond research agendas in order to capture the essence of the participants as a way of understanding and respecting data. Furthermore, doing research is about developing one's own research voice or way of thinking that is not bound by tradition, but instead by the meaningfulness of the study:

> *I have discovered that through utilising an emergent design the researcher is in charge of finding his/her own voice in the study. While positivist or single paradigms encourage the researcher to adopt a particular voice, an emergent design can encourage the researcher to develop his/her own voice. By developing one's own voice, the researcher can begin to go beyond the limits imposed by another's way of doing things in order to develop a more in-depth way of understanding and reporting the experience.*

(Horton Merz 2002: 150)

Developing a conceptual framework

Let us consider another scenario: Deborah is intending to investigate retention rates of students on her 'Access courses in Business Studies', in a college of higher education. Having researched the literature on Access Studies, Deborah has several ways of proceeding with developing a theoretical framework. She experienced great difficulties initially and it took quite a long time before she was able to set boundaries to her enquiry. During this 'finding her feet' stage she felt frustrated and quite unhappy. This was partly because she found everything she read very interesting and potentially worthwhile, and partly because the more she read the further she seemed to get away from her original research questions. It became increasingly important to look at her own context and her initial research questions which had led her to want to study for a doctorate in the first instance. Her college is located in a rural community with many students. She decided to research the notion of *rural education* as one of the concepts to develop further. Subsequently, she became increasingly interested in *gender* and *class*, concepts she had previously dismissed as irrelevant, but in the course of reading and reflection she realised that she had many women on her courses who were hoping to go to a university. She noticed that some students were developing a strong identification with other students of higher education and how they learned from one another. She then decided to look into *identity* as a theoretical concept together with other concepts such as *learning* in a rural community, gender and identity in her literature review and place these alongside the notion of *communities of practice* provided by Lave and Wenger (1991). This way she succeeded in developing a theoretical framework that was relevant to her own context and research questions.

This searching and questioning may take a long time. It may help you to develop a mind map, to have a flip chart handy in your area of study, or to pin a paper on a wall so that you are forced constantly to rethink your ideas and examine the *concepts* and the *conceptual/theoretical framework* you want to use. Some scholars may argue that the definition of concepts is a futile pursuit since they shift constantly and mean many different things in different contexts. It is argued that within the post-empiricist, post-modern approach the quest for essential definitions rarely furthers understanding, mainly because definitions arise in different contexts, locations and places in time. Furthermore, definitions can be political constructs and used for a range of different purposes. One just has to remember the many different terms that have been used for a range of different purposes, and over many decades, with regard to adult education (for example, continuing education, community education, recurrent education, post-compulsory education, lifelong learning). Concepts therefore offer ways of looking at the world which are essential in defining a research problem (Silverman 2001). You may know many other examples in your own area of work where concepts that were widely used a decade or so ago are no longer in use or whose meanings have shifted in the course of time.

Within a piece of educational research leading to a professional doctorate it is indeed advisable to be specific.

Conceptual clarity is an essential methodological tool – essential, that is, if research is to be rigorous. Yet it is a tool that many researchers do not use. Evidently they are unaware of its existence or they fail to master its use. It is not the easiest of tools to use, but worth taking time and effort to get to grips with because when it is properly used, it opens up many avenues into advanced research practice.

(Evans 2002: 49)

In other words, ensure that you have looked at a range of different meanings of the concept you want to use, determine which one is most appropriate in terms of your research, and then be consistent in your written work. If ambiguities persist then point these out. Furthermore, make this process transparent to the reader. Otherwise the whole process of data collection, analysis and dissemination is likely to be perceived as flawed. It is important therefore to understand the process as a whole, beginning with your initial research questions to the writing up of the thesis. Gina Wisker, an EdD supervisor, offered the following guidelines during an EdD seminar:

> *Your conceptual framework is the scaffold, framework of ideas, questions, and theories, methodologies and methods, which help you ask your questions, develop your ideas, underpinning your research and dissertation. It keeps you focused and on course, ensures what you find/conclude is underpinned by questions, theories, enabled by methods, arises from them and goes some way to addressing them.*

(EdD Research Seminar)

Discovering your own voice might be a useful way to end this rather complex chapter. In the end, you are encouraged to take from other people's theories what you think is meaningful to you in terms of your own research and your personal preferences and beliefs. It is part of your learning process, a way of gaining confidence about doing research, and relating findings to yourself, your own context and the situation in which you find yourself.

Here are some practical tips you might want to consider when developing your conceptual framework:

- **Develop a mind map, using different concepts, subheadings, themes which flow in and out of your research questions at the core of the map.**

- **Have this map near your place of reading and writing; look at it regularly, amend, change, cross out as your thinking develops.**

- **Use colour coding for different theoretical themes, concepts you are developing.**

- **Think about the relationship between, for example, your research questions, your reading, your conceptual framework and methods/methodologies you want to explore.**

- **Revisit your map from time to time. This means going back to the beginning and tracing what you have achieved. It is easy to be too ambitious and to lose oversight.**

- **Have this mind map in your head; carry around a notebook so that you can make changes as they occur to you.**

- **Set your boundaries: make explicit to the future reader of your research why you have included some concepts/theories and excluded others.**

- **Be consistent: provide an argument for the way you understand the concepts you want to use and why other interpretations may not be relevant to your research.**

As you will have noticed, designing a research project and developing a conceptual/theoretical framework is not only about the subject matter of your research or about the methods you are going to use but also about you as an individual: the kind of values you have and the world in which you believe. It is for this reason that we often stress the words *you* and *your* research. In the course of your study you will receive a great deal of advice, not only from your supervisor but also from fellow students, books and articles you read, research workshops you attend and, of course, the advice we offer in this book. Ultimately, however, it is you who have to make decisions, you who have to take responsibility for action and you who have to submit to an assessment process in order to succeed. Your final thesis will say a great deal about your achievements and your ideas about educational values and research.

6 Methodological Considerations

The previous chapter looked at how a theoretical framework could be constructed in terms of your overall research design. This chapter takes you a step further. It discusses yet more theories but this time those that influence your choice and the methods you will use when collecting your data. You may have noticed in your reading that many researchers describe research projects in terms of qualitative or quantitative methods such as interviews, surveys and observations among many others. They may then attempt to generalise their findings on the assumption that these can be applied in similar contexts elsewhere. Rarely, however, do they discuss the more philosophical dimensions which underpin their research. Yet as researchers they have personal preferences and beliefs about the nature of research itself and what it can achieve. As a research student, you will have to make your own position more transparent, usually in your methodology chapter. After all, the reader, or potential examiner, will want to know and understand your research methodology, that is, your thinking behind certain choices you have made and the links you have established between the research questions you have raised, the way you have gone about gathering your data and the conclusions you have reached. Your research methodology is rather like a fine thread running through everything you have thought about and done in the course of your research.

It is important, therefore, that you look at some methodological issues so that you can evaluate those discussed by others on the one hand, and then on the other focus on the ones that best suit your research questions, professional context and personal preference. In other words, it is only after you have looked more deeply into the various aspects of methodology that you can set your own boundaries in terms of research design and strategies. This chapter, therefore, will discuss the following:

- **what is meant by methodology?**

- **paradigms in educational research;**

- **qualitative or quantitative research? Overcoming the divide;**

- **research approaches: case studies, action research and surveys;**

- **aiming for rigour: reliability and validity.**

What is meant by methodology?

Writers of research methods texts generally distinguish between three interrelated categories:

- *Research methodology:* **this refers to general approaches to studying research methods (Silverman 2001).**

- *Research approaches:* **these are sometimes referred to as families or main methods and include case studies, action research and surveys.**

- *Research methods:* **these are also referred to as techniques, tools, instruments and even sub-methods, and include interviews, observations, narratives, questionnaires and documentary analysis.**

Research methodologies, therefore, comprise the theoretical frameworks and concepts in which approaches and methods are situated; they provide the rationale and justification (intellectual, epistemological and ethical) for the methods that are selected and the ways in which they are used (Stierer and Antoniou 2004). Cohen et al. (2004) offer yet another definition:

> *We return to our principal concern, methods and methodology in educational research. By methods we mean that range of approaches used in educational research to gather data which are to be used as a basis for inference and interpretation, for explanation and prediction ... the aim of methodology is to help us understand, in the broadest possible terms, not the products of scientific inquiry but the process itself.*

(Cohen et al. 2004: 44–5)

You will find many other explanations and definitions on reading further around this topic. However, before we can pursue the discussion on developing a deeper understanding concerning methodology we need to tackle two more important concepts: *ontology* and *epistemology.* They relate to the conceptions of social reality and are often confused, yet they imply entirely different ways of looking at research together with explicit or implicit sets of assumptions.

Ontology refers to the kinds of things that exist. For example, in the social world is it only individual people who exist, or socio-historically located interactional processes that exist, or can we also say that social groups and institutions exist, and if so what does this mean and what are its implications? Margaret Thatcher's famous denial that society exists is an ontological claim. Ontology, therefore, is described as the study of being and everything involved with beings such as human relationships and the ontological worlds they create. Many people starting in research are concerned with establishing what they consider to be the 'reality'. The questions therefore arise whether reality is the result of an objective nature or the result of individual cognition: is it given 'out there' or is it created in our own minds?

The second set of assumptions is of an epistemological kind. It concerns the very bases of knowledge. One can ask: is knowledge hard, real and capable of being transmitted in tangible form, or is knowledge soft, subjective, and based on experience and insight of a unique and essentially personal nature (Cohen et al. 2004). The most fundamental epistemological question is whether or how we can know anything. The term epistemology is derived from the Greek words *episteme*, which means knowledge, and *logos*, which means theory. It is the branch of philosophy that addresses the philosophical problems surrounding the theory of knowledge. It answers many questions concerning what knowledge is, how it is obtained and what makes it knowledge. It is a term you are likely to come across in your readings, particularly in the context of professional knowledge in education. You can ask, on what kind of knowledge is your research based, how does knowledge influence your research, and how is it developed on the basis of knowledge gained during the research process?

Paradigms in educational research

Concepts such as ontology, epistemology and methodology provide researchers with a shared understanding about educational research and the individual researcher's preferred place in what is often described in terms of a paradigm in educational research. A paradigm can be seen as a set of beliefs that deals with ultimates and first principles. A paradigm, it is argued, presents a world-view that defines for its holder the nature of the 'world', the individual's place in it, and the range of possible relationships in that world. These beliefs are basic in the sense that they must be accepted simply on faith (however well argued); there is no way of establishing truthfulness. Such debates may seem daunting at first and they may not seem that relevant to your research. Yet they cannot be ignored.

The notion of paradigms with, at times, overlapping conceptual boundaries has been widely debated over a number of years. It remains a contested area within the philosophy of research. Nevertheless, it is necessary for researchers to have a grasp of these discussions, even if some of these are dismissed in due course. The most widely discussed paradigms are as follows:

Positivism: This is a view of the world that deals with assumed certainties and 'reliable facts', which leave less room for doubt. Positivist research usually employs 'quantitative' statistical methods, and claims to provide 'objective' scientific knowledge; most positivists believe that research should take the form of testing hypotheses against empirical data.

Post-positivism: This paradigm accepts that society is really imperfect, and that absolutes are difficult to establish, but it still strives for 'objectivity'. Post-positivist research often combines 'qualitative' (non-numerical) and 'quantitative' (numerical) approaches to data collection and analysis. Post-positivists recognise that all knowledge is fallible, but nevertheless insist that it is possible to identify some knowledge claims as more likely to be true than others.

Interpretivism: This is a view which argues that there are no absolutes, but that all phenomena can be studied and interpreted in different ways, mainly because people and situations differ, and realities are not abstract objects but dependent on the inter-subjectivity between people. The key element of interpretivism is that it is defined or constituted in terms of human beings attributing meaning to, or interpreting pheno-mena under investigation. The role of communication, symbols and language is funda-mental to social life from an interpretivist's point of view.

Critical/constructivist (feminist): Research in this paradigm is critical of both posi-tivism and interpretivism in relation to social issues – although, just to complicate matters further, not all 'critical' research is constructivist, and not all feminist research is either 'critical' or constructivist! It is a viewpoint, reflected in research, that does not accept the socio-political status quo but seeks to challenge issues related to gender, for example, or to racism, power and all forms of oppression. It seeks to provide greater understanding and an explanatory framework of inequalities. Constructivist theorists argue that researching/learning is an active process in which researchers construct new ideas or concepts based upon their current/past knowledge.

Postmodernism: This paradigm seeks to break down conventional boundaries, and argues that locally limited, situational narratives are now required instead of 'grand theories'. Postmodernist approaches shy away from presenting the world based on rational progression though we can expect that life will be different in some way. There is a sense in which some postmodernists deny that fixed boundaries actually exist: the task is not so much to break them down as to draw attention to how permeable and movable the boundaries can be.

This is how one EdD graduate explained her thoughts about methodology in her thesis:

> *At the outset of my research study I felt a false confidence that exploration of my approach was in some-way unnecessary; after all, I wanted to explore what people thought about something so this would nat-urally lead to certain approaches and methods. However, part of the research experience is to problematise the apparently unproblematic, so it became important to scrutinise the possible approaches to my research. The literature does not, however, have a consistent way of referring to these approaches. For example, Guba and Lincoln (1998) refer to paradigms of positivism, post-positivism, critical theory and construc-tivism, Scott (1996) to positivism, post-positivism, and interpretive/hermeneutics, and Denzin and Lincoln (1998) to post-positivism, postmodernism and post-structuralism. These differences suggest that my approach may not easily fit into a category.*

(Barnett 2004: 48)

As Jean Barnett pointed out, discussion on paradigms is rarely straightforward. Some researchers see themselves firmly committed to one of these paradigms, for exam-ple, to the critical/constructivist one, others are quite happy to ignore such debates or move around several within the same project.

Qualitative or quantitative research? Overcoming the divide

From your perspective as an EdD student, much depends on the type of research you are undertaking, the overall research design and your own preferences, bearing in mind that your time for research will be restricted and your priority will be to link your research to practice in the field of education. Your research is likely to involve a mixture of research methods such as interviews and questionnaires, or observation and keeping a reflective diary, which means that in terms of methodology you are likely to cross what some perceive as the qualitative and quantitative divide. It does not seem that long ago that some researchers challenged positivist assumptions which in turn led to the juxtapositioning of qualitative over the quantitative methods, or vice versa. However, most researchers nowadays, particularly those in education, tend to be more pragmatic by mixing and matching according to needs and preferences.

To give an example: if you are interested in just how many classroom assistants are employed in the whole of the UK and how many hours they work, you are likely to want to use a quantitative survey approach within one of the positivist paradigms, which would involve the use of a questionnaire, sampling strategies and statistical analysis and evaluation. But while quantitative work would necessarily be positivist in terms of our earlier definition, it is not necessarily positivist in narrower definitions of that term, and some quantitative researchers specifically reject positivism. However, if the research questions ask how teaching assistants in a school cope with the various tasks they are asked to do, then you might choose an interpretive paradigm and qualitative research methods such as interviewing – although, conversely, it might be possible to identify different ways of coping and to study these via questionnaires, which may include open-ended questions, or through structured observation.

Roberts (2002), when a trainee researcher, states what while his PhD study was stimulating, challenging and an ideal conduit for exploring knowledge via discussion, argument and defence, he found the paradigm conflicts a bit confusing:

> To have the opportunity to explore method, methodology, epistemology, ontology and what may constitute 'acceptable' researcher practice is an enriching experience. I had previously heard of interpretivists decrying positivists et cetera, but I was unprepared to find quantitative researchers and lecturers openly dismissing qualitative approaches, and finding dismissals by qualitative researchers of the use of a quantitative approach; such are disappointing and confusing to the trainee researcher.

(Roberts 2002: 1)

Not surprisingly, an increasing number of scholars and researchers are against such demarcations. They consider 'paradigm wars' a waste of time. Instead, we should be concentrating on the development of better research skills and the understanding of all, not just a few, research methods. Combining research methods is, in any case, an everyday occurrence. Gorard (2002), for example, argues that the researcher should not ignore or avoid evidence because it might be the 'wrong' sort. There may be letters attached to uncompleted questionnaires from correspondents in a survey design, or pencilled comments in the margins of completed ones, which the researcher would not want to ignore, or when conducting interviews in a school, the researcher would not want to ignore school brochures received at the same time.

The multiple use of methods and thereby the mixing of paradigms therefore depends on the phenomena and questions under investigation. This multiplicity is best understood as a strategy that adds rigour, breadth and depth to the overall research design. In other words, one set of data the researcher has gathered by one method can be supplemented by an alternative one, as long as the rationale for each method is made transparent. Quantitative methods, for example, rely on heavily pre-structured approaches, while qualitative ones are based on the elucidation of interviewee opinions and perspectives, which means that the resulting data cannot be compared or integrated but simply used to complement, support or explain different kinds of data.

Mixing methods, however, is by no means unproblematic either, since both qualitative and quantitative methods have strengths and weaknesses that have to be recognised by the researcher. Be warned, therefore, in terms of your own research: you will need to critique a range of options, justify your choice and demonstrate how in turn the decisions you have made impact on your data collection, analysis and evaluation. Take the EdD student we have called 'Wendy', for example, and her research into access studies. She will be using questionnaires over a relatively large sample of students (about 200) and will follow these with 'in-depth interviews' with about fifteen students and three curriculum advisers, in addition to writing field notes and keeping a research diary. The methods Wendy has chosen are her own choice. She might have opted for 'observation' as a method and dropped the 'questionnaire' altogether, with predictably different outcomes. In other words, researchers have considerable freedom in choosing methods and approaches (unless they are funded by external agencies, of course). Although freedom means choices, it also brings responsibilities towards the professional and academic community in terms of ethics and validity. It poses the question of what to do with the data you have gathered, how to analyse questionnaires, interviews or field notes, for example, and how to present and evaluate the data so that your findings become meaningful, not only to yourself – or the tutors/examiners of a professional doctorate course – but also to your colleagues and the wider academic community.

This is how Jean Barnett introduced her methodology chapter in her final thesis:

Research reports such as this dissertation inevitably make both explicit and implicit claims about knowledge. As a researcher, I have made a number of choices during the progress of the research study about the methodological approach, methods, research instruments, and the site of study. This chapter presents a justification of these choices. The first subsection presents a discussion of research methodologies and the argument that is made for an interpretive stance. This is followed by an overview of the qualitative/quantitative debate.

> *Subsequent subsections argue for the use of survey and case study approaches, using questionnaire, interview and diary methods. Finally, ethical considerations, including those relating to the site of the study, are discussed.*

(Barnett 2004: 48)

Jean, in her opening paragraph, tells the reader what she intends to discuss in this chapter and how this discussion relates to her findings. You can almost see how her discussion on methodology is developed and understand that she has had to tackle quite complex ideas which shaped the research she has undertaken.

Research approaches: case studies, action research and surveys

Jean, in the previous example, used the term *case study* because her research was located in one manufacturing company. In some studies, including hers, the main aim is to find out facts and to understand according to particular contexts in terms of location and period in time. Such research can be described as *case study* research. Alternatively, research can involve large-scale investigations such as demographic *surveys* involving statistical data. Other types of research are aimed at problem-solving and intervention, in which case an *action research* approach may be appropriate. Perhaps the point to remember here is that the terms 'case studies', 'action research' and 'surveys' do not refer to specific methods but to broader approaches which can involve the use of several methods such as interviews, observations or questionnaires. All have advantages and disadvantages; furthermore, all are cloaked in different schools of thought and have proponents who advocate this theory or practice, or another one, which can be difficult to disentangle. It is beyond the scope of this book to discuss these in depth or detail. The aim is to raise your awareness so that you can pursue these debates if they are of relevance to your research.

Case studies

Case study is a term you will have come across numerous times in your readings. Its main purpose is to provide evidence to support the claims you are making. Gillham (2000) offers the following explanation:

> *A case therefore can be an individual: it can be a group such as a family or a class, or an office, or a hospital ward; it can be an institution – such as a children's home, or a factory; it can be a large-scale community – a town, an industry, a profession. All of these are single cases; but you can also study multiple cases: a number of single parents; several schools; two different professions. It all depends on what you want to find out – which leads us on.*

(Gillham 2000: 1)

This is a very broad definition. A case study involves seeking different kinds of evidence, which are to be found within the case setting, to provide the best possible answer to your research question. Gomm et al. (2002) point to a number of variations in the specific form that case studies can take:

- **in the number of cases studied, and the role of comparison;**

- **in how detailed the case studies are;**

- **in the size of the case(s) dealt with;**

- **in the extent to which the researchers document the context of the case in terms of the wider society and/or historically;**

- **in the extent to which they restrict themselves to description and explanation, or engage in evaluation and prescription.**

Case studies can provide unique examples of people in real situations. Such studies can penetrate situations and offer insights not easily gained by other approaches. Not surprisingly perhaps, in case study research *contexts* matter. Historical, social, environmental, even political contexts help to explain incidents and issues of concern which form the background to the research. Contexts are a guide for those who read research outcomes so that they can understand where research questions are located and why the researcher has chosen this particular focus. Significant, too, in terms of research analysis are the *number of cases* and the *amount of detailed* information to be collected – again questions which often concern new researchers. How many 'cases' should I consider? How many schools should I visit? How many documents should I read or interviews should I undertake? Again, there are no easy answers. Much depends on the level of depth and breadth you want to achieve in your research. The fewer cases there are to be investigated, for example, the more data can be collected from each one. Most case studies are associated with qualitative research, mainly because information gathered is dependent on the researcher's interpretation. However, case studies often involve quantitative methods, i.e. the number of nurses, teachers, or children to be investigated. You can observe, collect and analyse documents, make notes, keep a diary, conduct interviews, or take notes of informal conversations (bearing ethical considerations in mind!). Everything is important, nothing is turned away.

Such studies refer to a holistic approach, involving the whole institution or organisation or, indeed, several. They tend to refer to the uniqueness of that organisation or the community in which the research is located. Your concern as the researcher is to accumulate *evidence*, evidence that will in due course provide answers to questions you have raised and support the claims you are going to make. Gillham offers the following advice for those pursuing a case study approach:

- You need to be organised, by sorting out types of evidence;
- You must be alert to the need of *multiple sources of evidence*. This does not mean talking to a lot of different people (although you should do that, and cross-refer) but you should look at different *kinds* of evidence: what people *say*, and what you see them *doing*, what they *make* or *produce* and what documents and records *show*.

(Gillham 2000: 4)

In the end, all of this evidence needs to be woven into a narrative account, presenting a chain of evidence, i.e. each key element or link in your account supported by or related to evidence of different kinds.

All of this leads critics of case study research to argue that findings from such studies are rarely generalisable, precisely because they are related to specifics, uniqueness, interpretation and subjectivity. However, Gomm et al. (2002) present a different point of view. They argue that generalisation is not an issue that can be dismissed as irrelevant by case study researchers. In one sense it can mean that researchers may seek to argue for the general relevance of findings they have produced. In another, case study research involves generalisation within the case(s) investigated. It is possible to argue, for example, that if the research involves several organisations and a large number of people (multiple case study) then the research outcome will be more generalisable than if it involves just one organisation and a few people working in specific localised contexts (single case study). But perhaps a point that should be borne in mind is the relevance of findings to professional practice and how useful they are to others in similar situations rather then their wider generalisability.

Action research

Just like case study research, action research is neither a method nor a technique. It is an approach or an umbrella term, which nevertheless has proved to be attractive to educators concerned with small-scale investigations because of its emphasis on practice and problem-solving over a particular period of time. Although action research is based on a number of different approaches, action researchers share the common aim of wanting to link research to practice, an aim which links those involved with participatory research and action enquiry. Action researchers are often interested in reflective practice, professional development and empowerment, and institutional change through democratic processes. In action research, data can be collected that then generate further issues and actions, which, in turn, are revised and acted upon again. Greenwood and Levin (1998) state that:

> AR (action research) is a complex, dynamic activity involving the best efforts of both members of communities or organisations and professional researchers. It simultaneously involves the co-generation of new information and analysis together with actions aimed at transforming the situation in democratic directions. AR is context-bound, producing practical solutions and new knowledge as part of an integrated set of activities.

(Greenwood and Levin 1998: 50)

Action research, not surprisingly, includes a whole range of approaches and practices, each grounded in different traditions, philosophical and psychological assumptions, pursuing different political commitments. In the main, action research describes a family of approaches to enquiry which is participative, grounded in experience and action-oriented. It can involve just one person, the researcher, or two or more persons (see Reason and Bradbury 2001 for fuller explanations and examples).

Surveys and sampling

The survey approach, like the case study or action research, is not concerned with a specific research method; instead it can include a range of methods such as questionnaires, interviews, or other suitable tools. It can be seen as the collection of data about a large number of cases. However, in common with other research approaches, survey research addresses issues such as access, ethics and professional values. Surveys can include documentary analysis or literature surveys, or other pre-selected artefacts, even structured or systematic observations. Because of the variety of methods and design that the survey can encompass, it is an approach that can be used to investigate a wide range of research questions. Surveys are often undertaken in market research, for example, or in the Health Service, or even in a large-scale population census. In broad terms, it is an appropriate method when systematic and comparable data are needed, which can be obtained directly from a relatively large number of individuals. Survey research, therefore, is the method of collecting data by asking a set of pre-formulated questions, in highly structured questionnaires, to a sample of individuals drawn as representative of the defined large group of people, so that findings can be generalisable to that population. Because surveys aim to be representative, the selection of individuals, the sample, carries particular significance.

Several criteria can be applied to the choosing of samples for survey research. It is not within the scope of this chapter to discuss all of these here; however, the two main categories relate to *probability sampling* and *non-probability sampling*. The former applies to a selected sample of respondents who are most likely to be representative of the type of person (or artefact) under investigation, which in turn would allow findings to be generalisable to a wider group of people. The key to probability sampling is that a list of all the members of the population to which generalisation is to be made is available and members are chosen to be included in the study in such a way as to represent the main forms of variation in the population. The most basic way of doing non-probability sampling (or simple random sampling) is where every member has an equal chance with every other of being selected.

While the findings of surveys are often reported in the context of relatively large samples across a large number of schools, or a variety of commercial or public-sector organisations, even the general public at large, it needs to be noted that the survey approach can also relate to a small number of respondents within a single case study.

The investigator could, for example, adopt a survey approach by using a questionnaire addressed to all or a selected group of members of staff within one institution or organisation (secretaries, for example, assistant teachers, or mature students). It is, therefore, a useful approach to be considered within the boundaries of your own professional context and in the context of your research (see Alridge and Levine 2001 for further explanations and examples).

Aiming for rigour: reliability and validity

Whichever paradigm, approach or method you choose, you may still have some kind of doubt. How do I know that what I am doing is the 'right way' of doing research? Is there such a thing as a 'right way' in, for example, the design of interview questions, devising observation schedules, or implementing action research strategies? In other words, you would have to ask: Is my research approach valid and/or reliable? Are my findings generalisable? Notions of *validity* and *reliability* are significant terms in the research methodology that can be addressed in several ways. The term reliability is often associated with quantitative research, and is concerned with precision and accuracy. It stipulates that if the same research were to be replicated elsewhere by others under similar conditions, it should lead to the same or similar outcomes. You can ask: would the researcher obtain the same results using the same procedures but on different occasions? There are a number of ways you could check for reliability; however, this is not always feasible or necessary, since retesting can invite further questions hitherto not discussed.

The term validity is, of course, crucial to any research project. Yet it is a complex term which is littered with controversy in the research methods literature. It basically tells you if you measure or describe what you set out to measure or describe. It looks for logical consistency and comprehensiveness in terms of the construction and content of your research. Validity, therefore, in terms of your EdD thesis, will involve the key questions you have asked and the answers you provide to these questions once you have done the research and presented your findings. Check, for example, if the title of your research actually reflects what you have done – a surprisingly common error. Ask yourself: do my interview questions relate to the literature I have discussed? And so on. If the project should turn out not to be valid, then the whole enterprise is worthless. Validity is relevant to both qualitative and quantitative methods (see Hammersley 1992; Cohen et al. 2004). While earlier versions of validity were based on the view that it was essentially a demonstration that a particular instrument in fact measures what it purports to measure, more recently validity has taken many forms. For example, in qualitative data validity might be addressed through honesty, depth, richness and scope of the data achieved, the participants approached, the extent of triangulation and the disinterestedness or objectivity of the researcher (Cohen et al. 2004). Honesty, depth and richness are powerful concepts to be considered.

The approach you will have chosen for your own investigation – it may be a case study, an action research project or a survey involving sampling and statistical data – will allow you, as we have discussed, to employ one or more research instruments or method which will help you fine-tune your data collection. Finding answers to questions you have raised and seeing complex theories applied in practice to 'real' contexts, issues and people can be immensely rewarding. The 'real context', however, revolves around the 'you' as the researcher and your position within the research you are undertaking. Going back to the previous discussion on research paradigms and methodology you can ask: Am I an 'insider' or an 'outsider' to my research setting? Is my research about 'uniqueness of experiences' and specific issues which surround the case-based, idiographic research or have I adopted the generalising, positivist position? As we stated previously, much depends on the questions that you have asked and on the context to which you refer. It is a question of scale, emphasis and balance.

When thinking about your own research and your own position within it you want to think about Schutz (1970) and his reference to the cherry tree:

If I recognise this particular cherry tree in my garden as the same tree I saw yesterday, although in another light and with another shade of colour, this is merely because I know the typical way in which this unique object appears in its surroundings.

(Schutz 1970: 118)

He continues to refer to the pre-experience of cherry trees in general, plants in general, and the 'objects of the outer world'. Schutz points out that we see the cherry tree as the same cherry tree despite variations in how it presents itself to us. However, there is another way of looking at your own cherry tree, your research: this relates to notions of what you are researching, and how you feel about your research, which can change dramatically even over relatively short periods of time. You will see your research in many different lights and this is after all how it should be. Bear in mind that only by probing deeper into many of the points discussed in this chapter, and having begun to collect and even to analyse data, that can you experience a real sense of excitement and reward – just like the admirer of the cherry tree, who presumably also enjoys consuming its fruit.

7 Collecting Data

Educational research is a complex and sophisticated process. The possibilities for research in all areas of education are extensive, providing numerous opportunities to make valuable contributions to practice. This chapter attempts to demystify some of the complexities of the research process through raising questions and reflecting upon how EdD students have resolved some of their own methodological issues when collecting data.

There are many different ways in which you can collect data. Making decisions about strategy and method will depend upon the questions you want to research. To help you decide what sort of research methods you might use we begin with an exploration of what counts as educational research and discuss qualitative and quantitative methods in the context of research design. Techniques of data collection used by EdD students within their professional context are explored. The chapter covers:

- **qualitative and quantitative research designs;**

- **bounding and focusing your idea;**

- **techniques for data collection;**

- **combining methods;**

- **developing a pilot study.**

When you decide to undertake an EdD the first issue you may have to resolve is what you want to find out about and why. You will also, no doubt, be asking yourself if the topic you eventually choose is going to be one that will be viable and will count as educational research. Will it contribute to new knowledge about teaching, learning, management, policy issues or other educational phenomena and, indeed, what counts as new knowledge and educational phenomena?

Making your research topic count as educational research will depend not only upon the theoretical and methodological issues discussed in the previous two chapters but upon the choices you make about qualitative and quantitative methods and the interpretation that you present of the social world within your own research setting. For the remainder of this chapter we will use the broad terms 'qualitative' and 'quantitative' to discuss the methodological implications for data collection in the research process.

Qualitative and quantitative research designs

Researchers using qualitative or quantitative methods set about doing research in different ways, yet exactly how different those ways are can sometimes be difficult to determine. Qualitative researchers view themselves as the instrument of data collection. Feelings, impressions and judgements are all part of data collection. Personal interpretation plays a major role in terms of understanding and analysing the data. Findings are often presented as verbal descriptions.

In terms of subjectivity, quantitative researchers attempt to prevent data collection from being influenced by themselves. Such methods tend to use established psychometric tests or standardised observation schedules to collect data and statistical methods are used to analyse the data and draw conclusions. The quantitative researcher attempts to understand the world as it is 'out there', independent of personal bias and values.

As you consider which approach is most important for your topic of study a part of that consideration will be about what you consider represents legitimate data in your research. Is it qualitative or quantitative or a mixture of both?

Whether you choose to use qualitative or quantitative methods in your research, or perhaps a mixture of both, each method chosen will have an impact upon you as a researcher, your research participants and how generalisable your data will be. While qualitative researchers often see themselves as the primary instrument for data collection, quantitative researchers attempt to prevent themselves from influencing the collection of data. In terms of participants, quantitative researchers may try to maintain a detached yet positive relationship while qualitative researchers often interact closely with those they study. Large-scale quantitative research means that generalisations across classes of people can be made. In qualitative research each school, individual or culture is likely to have an idiosyncratic set of values and beliefs thus making it much more difficult to generalise across cases.

The often intractable problem of choice of method and methodological implications is tackled by Holdaway (2000), who links methods of research and theory. He argues that methods of research must be designed to document adequately the richness and diversity of meanings people attribute to phenomena. Our methods should allow us to document the ways in which meanings are constructed, negotiated within particular social contexts and become regarded as taken for granted.

Burton (2000a) explores the use of case studies and debates whether a case is a single case or a series of cases. Is it an individual, a cultural group, an organisation or a country? She also tackles the problem of how case studies should be conceptualised: as empirical units or theoretical categories. The positivist view would be that cases are either given or empirically discoverable while post-positivists would argue that cases are theoretically and therefore socially constructed by researchers for the purpose of carrying out their investigation. Burton argues that while the case study is frequently associated with qualitative research she agrees with Ragin (1992) that the qualitative and quantitative dichotomy is not as wide as might be supposed. She cites Ragin's example of two researchers both undertaking case study research in one organisation. Both use semi-structured interviews to collect data. The qualitative researcher analyses the interviews by coding text while the quantitative researcher codes the data with a view to producing a dataset which can be statistically analysed. Both undertake case study research and produce valid data but each would describe the process differently. The flexibility of case study research means that it can include numerical measurement where appropriate. Some research designs include more than one case study while data can be collected from documentary sources, letters, direct observation and participant observation. If you choose to use case study in the design of your research you will need to be clear about your definition and give reasons for your choice.

However carefully you design your research, it will seldom be straightforward and logical. Burgess (1994) explores the way researchers have been concerned with the messiness of research and the way methodological problems can be resolved in projects. He focuses upon the research process and its relationship with research design, data collection and data analysis and identifies a number of issues that researchers should consider when conducting qualitative research. In particular, he argues for flexibility in research design so that researchers can conceptualise and reconceptualise their studies.

Whether you intend to use qualitative methods or quantitative methods it is important to have an appreciation of both. You will need to interpret and evaluate the quality of publications that use a wide range of methods as you proceed with your literature search. Burton (2000b) provides an overview of the main design issues involved in survey research. She argues that it is misleading to perceive survey research as a linear and straightforward process as in reality it is fraught with tensions. We have summarised the issues that she identifies as follows:

- **The definition and operationalisation of concepts.**

- **The suitability of particular indicators that reflect a specific concept.**

- **How do you select a survey design?**

- **What are the benefits of combining quantitative and qualitative methods?**

- **What are the ethical concerns in terms of protecting respondents?**

- **Have you been realistic and taken account of personal safety in your research design?**

- **How do you address criticisms of survey research?**

As will be evident by now, the choice of methods is only the beginning of the research journey. Documenting that journey and the decisions that need to be taken are all part of being able to provide a reflexive account of the research process. In the next part of this chapter we will look at how you can bound and focus your initial idea so that your research design will have clear boundaries.

Bounding and focusing your research idea

Ideas, and thoughts about how to research them, can occur at any time, and therefore keeping a research journal is extremely important. Wield (2000) describes how Pam Smith, now Professor of Nursing at South Bank University, used her journal:

Research Journal extract

It was the early eighties. I was working as a nurse teacher in a care of the elderly hospital (actually it was still called 'geriatrics' at the time). I was struck how variable the students' experiences were, depending on which ward they had been allocated to. I commenced my journal in March 1983, and I began by looking at the relationship between students' educational needs and ward practice. I wrote:

Fundamental questions: how much does ward practice reflect classroom teaching? How realistic is classroom teaching in relation to practice? Is there a conflict between the two? If there is a conflict, how do students experience that conflict?

Learners frequently complain about the ideal and reality of classroom and ward. I ask them to give me some examples. They mention the Norton pressure sore risk calculator which we teach them to use in the school and is never used on the ward.

Even little things like bed-making – how in the classroom they're taught to put a tuck in the blanket to give patients room to move their feet, but this again is rejected by ward staff as impractical. They also feel awkward talking to patients even though we spend a lot of time in class discussing communication and interpersonal relationships. As for the nursing process, ward staff say there is neither time nor sufficient staffing for patient allocation. It seems important to try to unravel why there is this discrepancy. Ward staff must have their reasons? In the meantime students are caught in the middle of a seemingly impossible dream.

The head of the nursing school is concerned because she is expecting a GNC [General Nursing Council] visit in the near future and there is much written in the nursing press about proposed changes in nurse education in the next few years. Students in this school of nursing get a lot of responsibility very early too and they experience great anxiety if they're having to implement ward policy they don't agree with. Need to look at Isabel Menzies' study to check how she thought student nurses managed anxiety.

Someone told me about Anna Dodds' thesis, an in-depth qualitative study which looked at student nurses' ward learning experiences. They seemed to have had a really rough time. There are also a couple of recent studies – Fretwell and Orton – which examine ward learning and the ward sister's role. They also develop characteristics of the good and less good ward learning environments. Must get hold of these.

(Wield 2000: 8)

Pam kept a journal not only to capture insights about her research but also to document other events external to the research which affected her reflexivity. In her journal she discusses possible research interests and the current factors which influenced her thinking. These factors included concern about the literature, and about national and local concerns with the quality of nursing care and nurse education. Through reflecting on these issues she is able to move her ideas forward and begin to shape more clearly her research questions and the boundaries of her research. This is the time that we find out if our idea is too big to study with any degree of certainty or if the topic is overwhelming with too much and too vague literature, unclear methods and a bewildering mixture of theoretical perspectives. If ideas can be formulated into research questions or hypotheses that can be researched in a project then we can begin to assume that it will be workable.

When formulating researchable questions we are examining the very nature of ideas and where they came from. We examine the relationships between ideas, research questions, approaches and methods and the paradigms on which they are based. The research questions, therefore, are the link between the theory and practice of research. Formulating the research question determines the research approach, the literature, the data collection and analysis. However, as we discussed earlier, research is not a linear process. Each stage of the research will challenge an aspect of the research focus or methodology and lead to some re-evaluation of direction. As Holdaway (2000) argues:

> *Our questions must therefore sensitise us to discover the range of meanings attributed to a subject of interest, to the contexts within which the same meaning might change, to their relevance to action, and so on ... The cardinal rule is to be sensitive to and faithfully describe the commonsensical world of others, which for the social scientist means as minimal an intervention into their life as seems practical and possible.*

(Holdaway 2000: 165)

Our research questions, once formulated, will initiate the approach to the research methods to be used and the techniques for data collection which we explore next.

Techniques for data collection

Selecting a sample

Whatever approach you take to your research there will be elements of sampling and selection involved in the choices you make about participants, places and focus. If you are interviewing you will have to make a choice about who will be interviewed, when and how the interview will take place. If you are going to conduct observations you will have to decide who to observe and when it is most appropriate to carry out those observations. How will you decide on who should be interviewed or observed? Why should it matter who you choose? If, for example, you worked in a large secondary school and wanted to know more about the attitudes, behaviour and background of your pupils it is unlikely that you would be able to send a questionnaire to all the pupils who attended that institution. So, would you locate yourself in a central position in the school and then interview the students who passed you? Would you go into the communal eating area and interview the pupils there? Or would you select those pupils who attended your classes? It will, of course, depend on whether you want to generalise your findings to the whole pupil population in your school and, if you do, then none of the three sampling strategies above would provide you with a representative sample. The reason it would not be representative is because your choice of sample would depend upon availability, location or particular sets or groups of pupils and would, therefore, be biased. In setting up your research sample you should ensure that you do everything possible to limit bias.

There are two main sampling categories: probability sampling and non-probability sampling (see Chapter 6). Probability sampling is used when the researcher wishes the respondents to be representative of the type of person (or artefact) under investigation, which in turn would allow findings to be generalisable to a wider group. In this context, the researcher has control over the inclusion of individuals and criteria applied to the sampling frame. However, in non-probability sampling (sometimes known as opportunity or accidental sampling) control is denied to the researcher and the research is more open-ended with uncertain outcomes.

An EdD student exploring team working in two secondary schools described the reason for her choice of research sample:

Sampling for the study was done on a non-probability basis in the sense that the researcher targeted particular groups, in full cognisance of the fact that individuals in the groups might not be representative of the populations of Schools A and B in the statistically exact sense ... It was not the aim of the study to evince 'grandes generalisations'. This notwithstanding, the choice of groups to be involved in the study was purposive in terms of what this researcher judged to be typical of the types of teams which operate at the middle belt of secondary schools.

(Asong 2005: 57)

In the above example, Sophina Asong sets out to limit bias by acknowledging that the respondents would not be representative and therefore she would not have such tight control over the outcomes of the data. She goes on to explain:

Because what was being looked at by the research was team interaction itself rather than the similarities between pastoral and curriculum-type teams in different schools, it was judged more ethically sound to work with Team 3 School B (which is a middle level cross curricular Key Stage 3 co-ordination team), than to try to shoehorn participation from members of a pastoral team, whose initial unwillingness might have affected the quality of the data to be collected. The decision about the size of the sample (four rather than say ten teams) was imposed by the need to circumscribe the scope of the study while providing enough variation in data within and between schools such that comparisons and correlations were visible, but manageable enough to enable depth in analysis.

(Asong 2005: 58)

This EdD student made her decisions about her sample based on both ethical and practical reasons. The key point in her selection of a sample is that she is able to justify and explain with sound reasons the choices that she made. The boundaries to the scale of the study provide the final justification for sample selection.

However you decide to select your sample, it is important that you reflect upon the idiosyncracies of the sample you obtain (Pole and Lampard 2002).

Observation

Observation is something that you do a lot of the time as you go about your daily work, attend social occasions and enjoy your leisure activities. Teachers observe pupils and vice versa. Medical professionals observe their patients and patients observe those who care for them. All these activities in which observation is taking place are about far more than simply seeing what is happening; as we see we interpret, contribute, analyse and make judgements. As Pole and Lampard (2002) suggest, observation can be defined in terms of experiencing social phenomena: it is about hearing, feeling, enjoying, fearing, interpreting, talking and sharing. The problem for the observing researcher is how to capture these events through the observations that are made. You may be considering using observation as a research method in your own study and so you will need to consider carefully what it has to offer you and what will be the value of your observations. What are the range of observational strategies available to you as a researcher?

Distinctions between types of observations are linked to the degree of participation in the activities being observed. Gold (1958) identified a typology of four participant observer roles, ranging from the complete participant to the complete observer. Researchers who undertake the role of complete participant are usually conducting covert research while the complete observer keeps interaction to a minimum. In the middle spectrum of Gold's typology lie the participant as observer and the observer as participant. These categories are useful in terms of positioning the researcher and providing a viewpoint from which to reflect and analyse the data. However, observation has many complexities and you will need to think through carefully the type of observations that you wish to make and for what purpose.

In her EdD thesis Cheri Logan explains her reasons for using observation alongside other methods of data collection such as interviewing. She says:

> *I was interested both in what people had to say about graphic design understanding and in gaining purchase on the unarticulated meanings that might emerge in their daily knowledge transactions and operations, so it seemed that these means would complement each other well.*

(Logan 2005: 61)

Knowing what to observe, how to observe and when to observe are decisions that all researchers using observation will have to make. There are ethical issues of transparency and trustworthiness to consider as well as the danger of bias from the standpoint of the observer. There are a number of safeguards that you can use to ensure your observations are planned in an ethical and reliable manner, as shown in the box.

Planning	Allow plenty of time when planning an observation schedule. You will need to consider and address questions of access, bias and ethics.
What sort of observation should you undertake?	Structured observation schedules may provide boundaries to what you need to observe. An open-ended schedule, however, allows you to collect a wealth of detail and may allow new data to emerge.
Where and when to observe?	Some negotiation with your research participants about when observations can take place may be necessary and the location and timing agreed in advance.
Testing out your observation schedule	It is essential to try out your observation schedule to eliminate problems with the schedule.
Know what you want to observe!	Memorise your observation categories so that you can focus on the process of observation.
Video observations	If you use video as an aid to your observations then you will need to remember that once a camera is positioned it gives a fixed perspective of what is being observed. It might also be a hindrance if those being observed know it is there.
Recording observations	Keep recording schedules, checklists and charts simple and easy to use.
Writing field notes	When observing, write down exactly what you think you have observed and in another column write why you think this happened. Read field notes again immediately after completing an observation and add any further thoughts and impressions.
Shared observations	Observing with another person and comparing notes afterwards can be very helpful in eliminating bias.
Using other research methods alongside observation	Collecting data through different methods is important as it will help you to verify which data is relevant and worthwhile and strengthen your data analysis.

The list of safeguards may appear daunting but observations can provide a very rich source of data and allow you to access unarticulated meanings. Of course, observations of social interaction can provide many meanings and this is also part of the richness of observation. It may be more time-consuming than other methods, more lonely, more frustrating and more difficult, but the resulting data will provide a unique, vivid and in-depth portrait of the social context under investigation.

Interviews

If you choose to use interviewing as a method of investigation you will find that you are talking as well as listening to your interviewees. There is a wide range of interview strategies that you can select from that includes highly structured interviewing to informal conversations that allow you to reflect on answers and probe for further information. Interviews not only provide information, they reveal attitudes and opinions and sometimes confidential details that require sensitive handling. Interviews may be one to one or involve larger groups as in focus group interviewing. Whenever and wherever your interviews take place you will need to remember that the social construction of events or phenomena that emerge are constrained by the circumstances in which the interview has occurred. As a researcher you will need to recognise these constraints and take account of them in your analysis of the data. Interviews are unique, socially constructed and context-specific and this is both the advantage and disadvantage of the interview as a research strategy.

Interviews are often categorised as structured or unstructured (Burgess 1984a) but how will you decide what is the most appropriate style for you? This decision will depend upon the topic you are researching, how many people you wish to interview, the access and location of the interviewees, and how much time and resource capacity you have.

Focus group interviews

Focus group interviews, which bring together a number of people (usually between 6 and 10) with a facilitator in order to discuss a particular issue, may be appealing. They provide quick and easy access to a number of interviewees and can allow you to collect quite a lot of data quickly. There are disadvantages to focus group interviews as they take the attention away from the individual and discussion occurs at a less personal level than in one-to-one interviews. Focus groups require careful planning and organising as a badly planned focus group meeting could have a very damaging effect on the sort of data you will be able to collect. Most focus group meetings are set up with a clear purpose and agenda and the session is recorded so that it can be transcribed later and analysed. This can be time-consuming and complex unless you have worked out a clearly identifiable way of recognising the different voices on the tape. Some of the advantages and disadvantages of using focus group interviews are set out in Table 7.1.

Table 7.1   Advantages and disadvantages of focus group interviews

Advantages	Disadvantages
Interviewees may become more relaxed and therefore reveal more of their opinions and emotions	Some group members may dominate the encounter and hence discourage others from expressing their views
Observation of group dynamics and interaction can provide important contextual data	There may be problems with the composition of the group even though they may have been selected in an identical manner, e.g. one group may be lethargic and dull, the other very lively
More economical on time than several individual interviews	Group discussion can be hard to manage
Allows you to collect a lot of data at once	Recording and transcribing data afterwards may be problematic

In weighing up the advantages and disadvantages, the key feature in your decision-making should be the appropriateness of the method for your research study.

Structured and semi-structured interviews

As with focus group interviewing, one-to-one structured and semi-structured interviews need careful planning and sound preparation. They may take place face to face, or via the telephone or internet. Structured interviews are tightly controlled by the researcher, with specific questions planned in advance. More loosely structured interviews may be used if you want to give your interviewees the latitude to talk about themselves and issues that connect with their own individual and unique experiences. If you are planning to make use of this kind of interview then it is particularly helpful to trial what you want to do and consider the following issues:

- *Access*: many institutions will require you to seek formal permission before interviewing members of staff or students. If your research is with young children you will need to seek parental permission.

- *Confidentiality and ethical issues*: you should inform participants how the information they give you will be safeguarded. The use of pseudonyms for colleges, schools, hospitals and places as well as for individuals can help to protect your research participants.

- *Outcomes*: your interviewees should know what you intend to do with your research findings. You might build in the opportunity for them to see notes and transcripts before the data is made available to others or provide them with a copy of your research data.

- *Location*: where you interview your research participants will be important. It needs to be somewhere conducive in terms of the research you are doing and you should ensure that it is not stuffy or noisy with bad seating or lighting.

- *Language*: the questions you ask should be posed in a language that will be fully understood by the interviewees and should be asked in a logical order.

- *Questions*: you should begin with questions that can be answered easily and put the interviewee at ease. The questions that follow should be open-ended, allowing interviewees to express their views and opinions, and at the end of the interview any loose ends should be tidied up.

- *Note-taking:* whether you tape-record or make notes of the interview, it should be done in as unobtrusive a manner as possible.

- *Prompts*: you might want to use cards containing scales or ranges of predetermined responses or perhaps vignettes for the interviewee to comment on.

- *After the interview*: reflect and make notes about how the interview went. Your observation of body language, hesitations and other contextual factors will enrich your data.

The value of following up on interviews is described by Hazel Reid who researched careers advisers for her EdD:

Interviews were approximately 50 minutes long with follow up interviews of the same length. The value of follow up interviews needed to be weighed against the likelihood that respondents would want to improve on their original ideas, which then became reworked and could be viewed as either more considered or more contrived. I shared the transcripts with the participants after each interview, to ensure a degree of collaboration for the project. The only changes asked for by two personal advisers were minor clarifications following reflection on the first transcript.

(Reid 2004: 62)

The follow-up interview allowed Hazel not only to verify that the transcription was accurate, it confirmed that the view represented was agreed by the participants and provided transparency for both the researcher and the researched. This kind of feedback to the respondents may be especially relevant where the interview has been an unstructured narrative or biographical story linked to a career.

Unstructured interviews

For this type of interview you may have very few questions and thus allow the interviewee to develop a story or a narrative. However, such interviews do require great skill and usually last two to three hours as the narrative of an individual will emerge only gradually. If your research question is why did you become a nurse or a teacher or a manager it will require a great deal of reflection on past experiences, the influence of family and friends, where your respondents studied and early professional experiences. A whole personal biography is embedded in the research question. Arthur (2002) notes that this kind of in-depth research can be very revealing as participants become aware of their own views and attitudes because they may not have discussed or analysed their experiences previously.

Narrative or unstructured biographical interviews are rarely generalisable because they are about feelings, attitudes and individual life experiences. While other ethnographic approaches tend to focus on the present, life histories recall the past and as such belong to a broader social context that has become constructed over a period of time and draws on the hindsight of the narrator. The story that emerges will be a subjective account and interpretation of events. However, the value of narratives and life histories is that they allow the voices of those regarded as 'silenced' to emerge.

Survey questionnaires

Survey-based questionnaires are used in a wide range of research projects. They are often the starting point for a research project that later becomes narrower in focus. Whether you want to use a questionnaire as the main instrument for your data collection or as part of a range of methods, there are a number of issues that you should be aware of. First of all, you need to establish what sort of questionnaire it is that you want to administer. Bryman (2001) uses the term 'self-completion questionnaires' and in this kind of questionnaire the respondents answer questions by completing the questionnaires themselves. This is a useful term as it encompasses a number of ways questionnaires can be distributed. Self-completion questionnaires may be handed out and returned later to a collection point, they can be given out in lessons and collected in at the end, or they may be sent through the post or emailed to participants.

Giving out a questionnaire may appear a quick and easy solution to collecting data, and while it does have this advantage it will only work if the questionnaire is well designed. It can be very time-consuming to find that when your questionnaire responses are returned they have not elicited the information that you wished to find out. This may be because the questions were ambiguous, misleading, did not focus on the topic clearly enough, or used a style of language that the respondents were unused to. If you have ever thrown a survey questionnaire in the bin yourself perhaps now is the time to consider the reasons why you did! It is also too late, once your questionnaires are returned, to wish that you had included different questions. As a general rule, self-completion questionnaires usually:

- **have few open questions as closed ones are easier to follow;**

- **are designed in a way that is easy to follow so that respondents can comply with the instructions and not omit answering questions;**

- **are short, so that respondents do not become weary of completing the questionnaire and throw it away.**

Table 7.2 gives the advantages and disadvantages of using a self-administered questionnaire.

If you do decide to use self-administered questionnaires in your research make your questionnaire as precise and easy to follow as possible. Give a deadline for the return of the questionnaire and be prepared to send out reminders to those who do not respond. Remember, all this does take time, so you will need to plan for this in your overall research design and strategy.

Table 7.2   Advantages and disadvantages of using self-administered questionnaires

Advantages	Disadvantages
Cheap to administer and this is particularly advantageous if your sample is geographically widespread	You cannot collect additional data and it is difficult to ask a lot of questions
A quick way of collecting data. They can be distributed or mailed in large quantities	You may not always know who has completed the questionnaire and questionnaires may be returned with some questions unanswered
There is a lack of interviewer effect on the data such as bias in terms of gender, ethnicity or professional seniority	You cannot probe or prompt the respondent to give a more in-depth answer
There is no variability in terms of the questions being asked	Respondents can read the whole questionnaire before providing their answers. Some questions may not be relevant to all respondents
Respondents may find completing a questionnaire more convenient than arranging a face-to-face meeting	Response rates may not be very high. A 50 per cent response rate is barely acceptable in terms of providing research data. This applies particularly to postal questionnaires

Documentary evidence

Documentary evidence can come from many sources. It might be books, articles, photographs, diaries, letters, newspapers, magazines, physical artefacts (buildings/clothes), institutional policy documents, or national survey and census data on trends and activities of householders in Britain. In deciding whether a certain type of documentary evidence is appropriate for your research you should ask yourself four questions: Is it authentic? Is it credible? Is it representative? Is it meaningful? (Bryman 2001). Most research conducted by EdD students will involve a reference to documentary evidence and in some cases, such as an exploration of policies within a particular institution or school, documentary evidence may be the main source of data collection. Where you are using data that have been socially constructed you will need to consider the purpose for which that data were originally collected. Were they gathered for research purposes or for some other reason? Were they intended for a particular audience? How closely do the data match your own research agenda? All documentary evidence should be used only in relation to the context in which it was produced. When using documentary evidence in your own research you will need to ensure that the original purpose and reason for recording that evidence is transparent.

Documents represent attitudes, opinions and political directions that may be explicit or part of a hidden agenda. Documents may be considered to be objective when perhaps they or not. Analysing the discourse within documentary evidence presents a challenge to the researcher and uncritical use of such evidence could introduce a bias to your data that you had not intended.

Combining methods

Combining methods of research, or multi-strategy research, might seem an appropriate way of resolving the divide between qualitative and quantitative research. However, there is much debate about the combination of these research strategies both in terms of method and paradigm arguments (Bryman 2001). It would be easy to assume that by combining methods the advantages of each would be enhanced and the disadvantages minimised, but this may depend on whether this is encompassed within one research strategy, as, for example, using semi-structured interviewing within ethnography. The view that qualitative and quantitative research belong to two separate paradigms and research methods carry epistemological positions implies a commitment to particular versions of the world and knowing that world. Bryman proposes a 'technical version' of the nature of qualitative and quantitative research that gives prominence to the strengths of data collection and data analysis techniques. This version of the debate about combining methods recognises the distinctive epistemological and ontological assumptions but the connections are not viewed as fixed and unavoidable. Hammersley (1996) describes three ways in which multi-strategy research can be valuable. First, as a means of triangulation where results from an investigation employing one strategy are checked against results using a method associated with another strategy; second, where a qualitative research strategy is employed to facilitate research using a quantitative strategy; and third, where two research strategies are employed to access findings unavailable to the other, as, for example, where an ethnographer needs to employ a self-completion questionnaire.

A multi-strategy approach was adopted by Paul Redmond (2004) in his EdD thesis. He conducted a case study of the career aspirations and experiences of widening participation students and his overall research strategy was, therefore, a qualitative one. However, Paul needed to find out data that would help him to identify various 'positions' taken by widening participation students in relation to their motivation to enter higher education, their experiences while there and career orientations and aspirations. To do this, he devised a questionnaire based on Burke's (1998) 'career understanding template', which required students to respond to a series of career-related statements, as he argued:

It seemed possible that such a questionnaire-framework, if developed carefully in accordance to the research issues, might provide an insight into widening participation students' career-related positions.

(Redmond 2004: 74)

In designing his questionnaire, Paul had to make sure that the question fields related directly to the research issues in the study. He used a design matrix to check the research issues against the target data and the question number in the questionnaire. Through using this questionnaire he was able to explore aspects of the conceptual framework of his research study with larger numbers of students than would have been accessible to him in one-to-one interviews and focus groups. A multi-research strategy, used in this way, can be extremely useful for EdD students whose research, of necessity, may often focus on small-scale qualitative research.

Whatever research strategies you eventually decide to use there is always the necessity to trial your methods before embarking on your main period of data collection.

Developing a pilot study

Why is it necessary to undertake a pilot study before embarking on your main period of data collection? A pilot study, or initial study, allows you to try out the research techniques and methods that you wish to use and to see if they work in practice. It may be that you wish to pilot a questionnaire or try out an interview schedule that you are planning to use in your data collection. Alternatively, you may want to do documentary analysis or organise a focus group interview. In all these cases, the pilot study will help you to firm up your research questions and methodology. To make the most use of your pilot study you will need to plan it into your research right from the very beginning.

You may be working from the assumption that you really know what you are doing, but you should not underestimate the value of a pilot study. Even if you have conducted research before and used the methods you plan to use in your EdD, collecting data has a habit of turning out very differently if you are in a different context, different time and working on a different research project.

Your pilot study does not have to be huge. Trying out a questionnaire on a small group of three or four, or conducting two or three interviews or observations will give you a small amount of data that you can use to analyse and consider the kind of findings that appear to be emerging. As part of this analysis you should consider how long it took you to collect the data, and how long it takes you to analyse each observation or interview. Make a note of the length of your interviews. Did they last longer than you intended and did it take you a long time to transcribe data that you recorded? It usually takes several hours of transcribing for every hour of recorded tape! Will you need to reduce the scope of what you want to do in your research? Consider how well your data collection and analysis techniques work and if there are ways in which you can improve their effectiveness.

Having completed a pilot study you will probably find that you need to revisit your research plan and adapt your original intentions. You will be able to move forward confidently, though, knowing that you have tried and tested your research strategy and methods and that they inform your research question in an appropriate way.

Conclusion

This chapter has focused on qualitative and quantitative research design and techniques for data collection. When doing research it is essential to be able to state how you have arrived at your conclusions and how you have avoided bias in the process of data collection. A rigorous approach at this stage will be of enormous value as you set out to analyse your data, which we consider in the next chapter.

8 Analysing Data

Far more has been written about how to collect data than how to analyse it so it is not surprising that many new researchers find the task of data analysis daunting. The process of actually collecting the data can become all consuming and some EdD students discover, sometimes too late, that they have not given enough thought in the early stages of their research to how they intend to analyse their data or they have not left enough time to work on their data. Analysis is an integral part of the whole research process. The choice of research questions indicates the method that should be chosen and, in turn, the choice of method leads to a process of analysis that will help in understanding the social phenomena under investigation. The complexity of the relationship between data and analysis is explored in this chapter through considering:

- **where to begin;**

- **levels of analysis;**

- **analysing qualitative data;**

- **analysing quantitative data;**

- **being reflexive.**

Where to begin?

The analysis of your data in your thesis will form the largest part of the entire document. In a typical EdD thesis of around 50,000 words, you might reasonably expect the results of data analysis section to take three or four chapters. You will have a mass of data from your observations, field notes, notes in your personal journal or diary, interview transcripts and documentary evidence. You may also have some quantitative data from questionnaires that will need to be deciphered and set out in tables or charts before it can be used as research evidence in your thesis. However you decide to analyse your data, it is important that you can provide a rationale for your strategy within your thesis. Transparency in terms of how you both collect your data and apply the lenses that you choose to explain your findings is an essential component of valid educational research.

The answer, of course, to where to begin with data analysis is at the beginning when you are designing your research project. As Pole and Lampard (2002) suggest, analysis is both integral to and an inevitable aspect of the entire research process with a different level or form of analysis necessary at every stage of the research.

Levels of analysis

The notion of levels of analysis is a valuable one when considering how to manage the bulk of your data. It allows you to return to aspects of your data at different points throughout your research. In this way you will strengthen your analytical framework and may even uncover new ways of understanding your research findings. It is important that the procedure for analysis should be considered from the outset of the research project. Qualitative methodologies produce a mass of data and therefore need to be sorted and managed into what is useful for the project being studied. In order to ensure rigour and reliability this process needs to be well planned. Finch and Mason (1990) argue that a key way in which qualitative methods differ from quantitative methods is in the sampling or selection of people studied. In surveys, decisions are made at the beginning of the project and follow formalised statistical procedures for sampling. In qualitative or fieldwork methods such decisions are taken at various stages in the project on the basis of contextual information. Levels of analysis can be relevant, for example, when listening to interview tapes, making a preliminary assessment of each case, itemising and categorising characteristics and situations.

Finch and Mason (1990) identify a number of principles concerning analysis of data in the research process. They argue that analysis is constantly taking place and forms the basis for decisions about strategies linked to a particular theoretical perspective decided at the beginning of the research process. Preliminary forms of analysis, such as listening to interview tapes, are the basis upon which informed decisions are later made. Such early decisions are both situated and informed. However, the researcher needs to be clear about the principles underlying that decision, and the reasons for it. Decision-making while collecting data is part of the process of modifying and sharpening the theoretical underpinnings that are grounded in data. It also acknowledges the changing contexts of the investigation and the influences of others upon that investigation. The implication of this is that delayed decision-making becomes a positive part of the research process, giving the researcher more flexibility which taking all the decisions at the beginning of the research would not allow.

Working in this way can encourage you to be systematic as there is a continual need to explain the reasons behind your decisions and what the purposes and consequences might be. A key outcome of your preliminary analysis is that it will become cumulative if careful records are kept documenting the decision-making process, for example in a research diary. These records will be highly informative when you begin the process of formal analysis.

Analysing qualitative data

Collecting qualitative data generates huge amounts of words that can seem constantly to teem back and forth without any clear pattern emerging. So many words, of course, provide a very rich vein of data and ordering and shaping these words to draw out themes and issues can be both mesmerising and arduous at the same time. Mesmerising because it is tempting to become lost in the detail and arduous because you have to keep pulling yourself back to the task in hand and find a pathway through. Thinking about your analysis from the start of your project is one of the ways in which you will both find a pathway and keep on track. This is why earlier in this book (see Chapter 5) we have included a discussion about some of the issues, such as grounded theory, that are traditionally not discussed until the analysis chapter. We hoped that by doing this you would already have formed some of the concepts and skills you require to get to grips with the analysis of your research. If you are intending to use a grounded theory approach to analysing your data, you will need to familiarise yourself with some of the key reading on qualitative data analysis such as Miles and Huberman (1994) and Bryman and Burgess (1994), and more detailed elaborations of grounded theory by Strauss (1987) and Strauss and Corbin (1990; 1997). However, as Bryman (2001) suggests, grounded theory does have its limitations such as the practical difficulties of the time taken to transcribe tape-recorded interviews, and the issue about whether grounded theory actually results in theory rather than a rigorous approach to the generation of concepts. Grounded theory also invites researchers to fragment their data by coding it into discrete chunks and, as EdD student Paul Redmond (2004) discovered, this is not always helpful:

> *The research methods generated large quantities of data, so much so that at times the sheer quantity of data threatened to swamp the process. Grounded theory initially seemed to offer one way of dealing with this ... After experimenting with grounded theory when analysing data from the pilot interview, I became concerned that the emerging theory failed to acknowledge the implicit theories and conceptual framework which had guided, informed and structured the study. Like others ... I was anxious to avoid the analysis 'degenerating' into a 'fairly empty building of categories'.*

(Redmond 2004: 81)

Finding that grounded theory was not going to work for him, Paul chose to develop an approach to analysis elaborated by Bassey (1999) that was appropriate to research conducted through case study. He used several research methods, such as focus groups, interviews and questionnaires, all of which produced data that could have been analysed using grounded theory. However, he found that his themes emerged more clearly using a process whereby he stored his data electronically, using the software package QSR NUD*IST, and then wrote draft analytical statements based on his reflections on the data. In this way Paul was able to develop a coherent frame for his research where the research issues were drawn up with reference to the conceptual framework and through the literature review, which led to the collection of raw data. This in turn was reflected on, leading to the analytical statements and resulting in empirical findings. In Bassey's terms, such findings could lead to several applications such as 'fuzzy' propositions, reports, surveys or evaluations, or case reports.

Paul found that the emerging themes resulted in three key chapters on the analysis of his data in his thesis. His study focused on the career aspirations and experiences of widening participation students. The chapters that developed did not appear in a linear fashion but the richness of his analysis gave him three key themes: 'Outcasts or Lucky Survivors?'; 'Wash'n'Go: Widening Participation Students Experiences in Higher Education'; and 'Economies of Experience: Widening Participation Students and the World of Work'. This approach to his data analysis brought the writing up of his research to life and enabled him to produce an original and interesting study.

Paul chose a method of analysis that was appropriate for his research and there are several other ways that you might think about analysing interviews.

Analysing interviews

In terms of interview data analysis there are a range of approaches to analysing text. If you are exploring theories or concepts developed in other sources then your analytical approach will be predetermined. However, if you are interested in exploring interpretations and attitudes then a more grounded approach is required (Glaser and Strauss 1967; Strauss 1987; Burgess 1984a). The amount of unstructured data means that an organising system is needed so that the material can be broken down into manageable chunks that can be sorted. Stroh (2000) suggests that this is usually done through a coding procedure in which chunks of text are labelled, or coded, and then stored by these codes. However you might choose to carry out your coding, it will be important to be exact so that you can easily trace previous codings and make cross references in your data. Then the main task is to extract something meaningful from the information you have gathered. The meaningfulness will be determined by your research questions and your conceptual mapping within the literature review. When analysing data you should always be open to the element of surprise, for the 'something' that turns up in the data in an unexpected way.

Transcripts, field notes, or any other type of documentary material can all be dealt with in the same way. Usually this means going through the material with a highlighter pen, marking all the points that surprise you when you find them and those that come up repeatedly. This is a process that needs to be done several times and even when you think you have come up with a sound method of analysis it may not be one that your respondents either recognise or feel comfortable with, as Cheri Logan discovered in an early analysis of some of her data for her EdD.

Through observation and interview Cheri Logan researched the values, meanings and beliefs that informed teachers' and learners' views of design expertise in one under-graduate programme. Interpretation of the data was initially problematic and she tried several approaches before she adopted a framework for metaphor-based analysis. Of her initial attempts at data analysis she says:

> *Early interpretations included attempts to assign data to knowledge categories discussed in the literature, distinguishing conceptual and procedural knowledge (McCormick 1997); although I felt some 'forcing' was involved, I did manage to make a case for this interpretation in the pilot study report. However, the analysis did not ring true with tutors during respondent validation; they commented that it was a 'clever' and 'theoretical' example of 'education speak' but failed to represent their views of graphic design, and I felt the framework would take me no further. I also tried to use semiotic analysis, using ideas from knowledge literature on semantic chains (Cobb et al. 1997) and from methodology literature on semi-otics and fieldwork (Manning 1987). At one point, emergent theme analysis (see Rubin and Rubin 1995, Ch.10; Mason 1996, Ch.7) seemed to offer the best hope of making sense of the data.*

(Logan 2005: 69)

None of the above approaches to analysing data offered Cheri what she required in terms of her own research. Her analytic method emerged slowly and it was the records that she kept in her log that allowed her to track the process of her emergent analysis. She discovered that her tutor respondents shared discernible themes and used similar metaphors to describe them. From this finding she went on to develop her metaphor-based methodology and her metaphor analysis. She also shared her new approach to analysis of her data with her tutors and found that they responded positively to her empirical findings. Set out below is an example of her thematic analysis with emerging metaphors:

Summary of thematic analysis: tutor respondent

Interview B

Filename: anaffect(Works)
Baffect (floppy/rtf)

Theme 4: Affect
a) *What does Dave mean when he talks about 'affect' i.e. attitudes, feelings?*
   There are 4 discernible themes in the discussion:
   Pleasure, often conceived as physical and sensual
   Passion
   Mediocrity
   Learning as the finding of treasure

1 Pleasure

The respondent sees graphic design as an intensely pleasurable activity. Designers experience such satisfaction themselves and provide them for others by their ability to create physical changes in the world that 'make it aesthetically pleasing'. All working graphic designers should have this basic ability to reconfigure elements of the physical world in this way. The ability to create 'pretty stuff', though, is a limited one and more than this is needed for design expertise.

The effects of design on viewers are often described in physical terms, pointing to the sensual nature of the experience: liking and disliking is described as inducing temperature change (being cooler or warmer about a design), affecting the vital organs ('... made my heart sink') and being offensive to sight ('horrible, nasty, ugly things'). Studio activities by which design is carried out are also sensually envisaged, inviting physical contact ('I love the energy of the first year (projects). I kind of want to touch it.') and providing physical shock ('short, sharp projects').

It is expected that design work will provide pleasure and enjoyment, qualitative judgements about their worth rest on this ability and terms such as 'playfulness' and 'fun' are used to describe prized attributes of successful designs. Conversely, some designs while being 'enjoyable' are not 'exciting', lacking the ability to provide intense pleasure, they are therefore less highly regarded.

Metaphors: pleasure/enjoyment/excitement; feel/touch/sight/play/fun

(Logan 2005: 182)

Through recording and working on many extracts similar to the one above, Cheri found a way to analyse her data that she considered represented her findings in an authentic manner and which she found was recognisable and understandable to her respondents. A key issue evident in the analysis extracts from both Paul and Cheri is the extent to which the method for research and the process of analysis are intertwined. Each student had to find a way of understanding their data and analysing them that provided a response to the research question. Although both EdD students followed an individual pathway to resolve issues of their analysis there are a few key processes that they followed that are applicable to all qualitative data analysis:

- **look for patterns and themes in your data;**

- **think about your process of analysis right from the beginning;**

- **apply different levels of analysis to your data and keep returning to them again and again;**

- **try to draw the story out of your data by drawing themes together;**

- **explore how the use of metaphors can draw your data together;**

- **consider whether your findings are rare or common and be prepared to revise your categories and definitions as your research progresses;**

- **consider whether your analysis is developing your 'story' and helps to hold it together;**

- **think about whether your analysis arises out of your method of research, your research question and your developing findings;**

- **does your analysis link back to the issues that you drew out of your literature review?**

The processes of qualitative data analysis can be as unique as the methods of research and this is what will make your research data fascinating and interesting to work with as a researcher. It will also assist in providing you with an original approach to your research and provide a contribution to the field of knowledge in which you work.

Analysing quantitative data

To analyse quantitative data effectively you will need a range of technical skills and if you feel you need to brush up on some basic knowledge in this area then you would be well advised to study some key research methods texts such as Bryman (2001), Bryman and Cramer (2001) or Pole and Lampard (2002). In this section we will be considering some of the issues linked to quantitative data analysis and many EdD students in fact use a mixture of both qualitative and quantitative research in their studies.

There are a number of sources of quantitative data such as survey data in the form of questionnaires, but also observations made in classrooms, on playgrounds or in meetings can provide data that can be statistically analysed. It can be very helpful to represent data in a thesis in the form of graphs or tables to back up other forms of data collection and analysis. As with qualitative data analysis, the process should begin early with a consideration of the techniques you will use. One of the commonest mistakes in the analysis of quantitative data is to assume that it is a process that does not need to take place until all the data are collected (Bryman, 2001). While analysis of quantitative data does indeed typically happen at a late stage you do need to be aware of the techniques you are going to use for two reasons. First, you need to match the techniques to the variables that you have created in your research. Secondly, the size and nature of your sample will impose limitations on the techniques you can use.

In his EdD research, Paul Redmond used a mixture of quantitative and qualitative methods. On the quantitative side, he used a questionnaire to identify the career-related positions of the widening participation students he was studying. To help him to do this he used Burke's (1998) 'career understanding template', which provided examples of statements that students were asked to respond to about their careers. In designing his questionnaire Paul had to ensure that the question fields related directly to the research

Table 8.1   An example of a questionnaire design matrix

Research issues	Target data	Question number
(1) Factors motivating widening participation students to enrol in HE	Pre-HE qualifications; parents' education background; 'significant others'; family responsibilities; key factors	1, 2, 3, 4, 5, 6, 7, 8
(2) Widening participation students' experience of higher education: career aspirations and orientations	Work experience/ commitments; hours worked; extent to which positions have changed	9, 10, 11, 12
(3) Implications for careers service	Hours worked by students; type of current work; career orientations	All – specifically 10–13

Source: Redmond 2004: 74. Used with permission.

issues in his study. He used a matrix to ensure the research issues were properly addressed and the questionnaire was structured appropriately (see Table 8.1).

Paul worked through several levels of analysis with the data that his questionnaire provided. An early analysis of a pilot questionnaire allowed him to make adjustments to inconsistencies in a few of the questions and to sharpen those questions that were imprecise. This early trial of his questionnaire and analysis of data resulted in a clearer and more effective research tool. His amended questionnaire was sent to 150 students on courses in each of the academic areas he was studying. Sixty-seven were returned to him and he was able to collate these data via a spreadsheet from which he was able to draw up a number of tables and graphs.

Analysis issues

Qualitative and quantitative data analysis is concerned with identifying patterns, impli-cations, consistencies and inconsistencies in the data. How you will make this judge-ment will depend in part on the nature of your study and your own epistemological stance. You will need to demonstrate that your decisions surrounding your analysis are clear and that you can present your data concisely. Ensuring that it is relevant to your research ques-tion is important to keep in mind all the time, and will help you with the arguments you are developing. You will, no doubt, have more data than you need to make your argu-ment clear and you will have to decide what to put in and what to leave out. There is no point in including material that does not further your argument and provide coher-ence to your research. If you are clear and concise about the way you analyse your data you will also help to eliminate the problem of bias in your data.

Bias is an issue for both qualitative and quantitative researchers when designing and analysing a research project. We are all products of an environment that shapes and distorts our perceptions in subtle and numerous ways. The researcher who has an emotional stake in the outcome of the research, for example a doctoral student, is particularly susceptible to bias. Individuals may unconsciously slant their work in a hundred different ways, such as systematic errors in sampling, in selecting measures, scoring responses of subjects, the way respondents are treated, observations of performance, recording data, and in analysing and interpreting results, all of which may favour the desired outcome. Observer bias (Borg and Gall 1989) has been recognised as a problem for centuries in scientific research. Interpretative researchers have found that such biases not only exist but are much more subtle and complex than previously thought.

Analysing your data involves critical reflection as you make decisions about what you consider to be important. As you constantly work through different levels of analysis in your data you will consider your own attitudes, experiences, thoughts and perceptions of the processes involved in your own research. How you have collected and analysed your data will be evident in your final evaluation and writing up of your research.

Being reflexive

Seeking to analyse, comprehend meaning and be rigorous about issues of bias does not, of course, mean that the research process is devoid of reflection. Tesch (1990) argues that reflection is informed largely by intuition or what may be termed tacit knowledge. Shacklock and Smyth (1998) argue that reflexivity is an attempt to identify, do something about, and acknowledge the limitations of research in terms of the location, subjects, process, theoretical context, data and analysis. Reflexive accounts recognise that the construction of knowledge takes place in the world and not apart from it. They consider reflexivity to be the conscious revelation of the role of beliefs and values held by a researcher in the selection of a research methodology for knowledge generation and its production as a research account. The denial of the subjectivity of the researcher in the pursuit of objective collection of empirical data is discussed by Roman and Apple (1990) in their account of the 'missing researcher' and provides a strong case for the reflexive position. Reflexivity can encourage you to provide an honest and ethical account of your research. Such accounts provide a window for other research students to see how you have faced up to the challenges and dilemmas of enquiry. Your commitment to your research and those you are researching often causes dilemmas and tension in research relationships. How your research tale is written can provide insights for the experienced as well as the inexperienced researcher.

Taking an autobiographical approach to your research (Burgess 1984b) and recording events in field notes and diaries will help you to identify stages in your research and different levels of analysis. Coe (1994) explores stages of his development as a researcher evidenced through the field notes he kept. Making the field notes became a skill demanding continual reassessment of purpose and priorities and strategies about what to write. He comments in his field notes:

> *There seem to be at least three levels at which I react to my experiences in the nursery. The first seems to be immediate – jot down notes about what is said and done that address my research question. The second is at a level where I begin to pull back and make observations that interpret what is happening. For example, are there ways of helping in writing that are used by many children and teachers? The third is at a level where I think about what the whole thing means. And here I get hung up in my value system.*

(Coe 1994: 225–6)

Coe's account illustrates the complexities of ethnographic enquiry. He sees the research process as a spiral where the researcher passes between levels. If research is an ongoing process (Odell 1987), researchers are continually required to think and rethink their understanding of their discipline but also the research questions to be asked and the best procedures to analyse their work.

Conclusion

There is a sense in which research is never finished. Reflection will enable you as a researcher to see both the possibilities and the liabilities of your ever-developing reflexive and interpretative account of your research. How you can develop a reflexive account when writing up your research is one of the considerations of the next chapter.

9   The Writing Process

Writing is part of the ongoing process of developing a thesis. This chapter explores the different stages of writing throughout the research process and presents some practical examples of the ways in which you can develop your writing skills. The examples used are all drawn from the work of EdD students. This chapter will consider:

- **writing as a process;**

- **organising your writing environment;**

- **beginning writing;**

- **deciding the structure;**

- **setting targets;**

- **themes and concepts;**

- **style issues;**

- **negotiating feedback.**

Writing as a process

The writing process, like the research process, is not a linear activity. It can be messy and frustrating as drafts have to be rewritten or reorganised, and sometimes take an entirely different direction from that which you first intended.

This chapter aims to raise your awareness of the wide range of activities which combine to form the process of writing a doctorate – planning, structuring, drafting text, reading text, negotiating feedback, rewriting and editing. By the end of this chapter you will, ideally, have built on the techniques you already possess to improve your writing performance.

The writing process stretches across all the activities associated with completing your doctorate, from the initial planning and writing of drafts, the data gathering and analysis and the final thesis. Recognising that writing is part of the whole process of completing your thesis, and not something that you do towards the end of your research, will allow you to establish good writing habits from the start of your EdD.

While you are doing your doctorate you will, no doubt, be undertaking a variety of roles alongside that of research student – professional worker, partner and parent, to name three possibilities. You should also never lose sight of your other essential role, which is that of writer. Ward (2000) quotes one of his interviewees who says:

> This sounds a bit odd, but I never got the impression that writing up the thesis was the primary objective ... I got the impression that the idea was to do experiments and get the results out in presentations and papers, and the thesis would happen by itself. The thesis wasn't my focus. Nowadays as a professional writer rather than as a scientist, my whole focus is on what I'm writing. Now, when I get a writing brief, I immediately think about how the final piece is going to look.

(Ward 2000: 5)

The loneliness of writing may be one reason why some doctoral students put off the moment of putting pen to paper or opening up that blank document on the computer. Finding strategies to cope with this is part of the writing process. You need to find out what sort of environment is the most comfortable for you, or if your setting for work on your thesis is not conducive to writing you need to consider how you can work around this. How you structure your work and break it down into short-term achievable goals that fit in with the completion of drafts are skills that you need to develop as soon as possible. You will have to respond to feedback from your supervisor and consider how to take account of new questions and issues that you may not have included. The writing process is also an emotional process and it may be difficult to address changes when you feel you have laboured over a section of your thesis for several hours! Sensitive negotiation on both sides is an important part of writing a thesis.

As you read this chapter, remember that you are already a writer of some experience, otherwise you would not have reached this stage in your academic career. Now you need to consider how you can hone that experience to the writing of a thesis and find out what new skills you need to develop.

Organising your environment

To help you to become an effective writer you need to work out what kind of environment suits you. Do you know what your best way of working is? What might you need in order to maximise your writing output? Are there conditions that you simply have to put up with? How can you solve your problems? One solution was cited by an EdD student:

> *What I was left with was a huge dilemma facing all part-time researchers: how to analyse the myriad of data gathered, when I shared an office in which the 'phone never stopped ringing, and when, due to having six children (some still at the scribbling/ripping phase) I did not have a study at home. I was extremely fortunate in being able to call in the Teacher Fellow connection from 8 years previously and pay for use of a tiny box room in an Oxford College (without a phone!) for a couple of months to blue-tack data summaries around the walls.*

(Open University 2005: 10)

One discipline you will need to learn is how to deal with interruptions. Some things are obvious, such as turning down the volume on the answerphone or putting a 'Do not disturb' sign on the door. Ultimately, you need to find your own best way of writing and feel comfortable in that writing environment.

As you organise your environment it is also worth remembering that computers will not do everything for you and only form part of the writer's repertoire. Packages for checking spelling and grammar are not foolproof and can be cumbersome. You may find it difficult to word-process or find sitting at a computer limits your creativity. Using a computer will not necessarily make you a better writer and many writers still prefer to use pen or pencil and paper when writing a first draft. The act of writing and the tool that you use are all a part of who you are. Woods (1996) has argued:

> *Writing is not a mechanical, linear technical exercise simply of placing what is in one's mind on paper, the writing tool – whether pen, typewriter, word processor or whatever – merely being the recording device. It is a much more complicated activity in which the whole writer's self is engaged. Writing is an expression of the self. The writing tool, as an extension of self, is central to the psychological processes involved.*

(Woods 1996: 133–4)

Beginning writing

How and where do you begin writing? I have often used the phrase 'Don't get it right, get it written!' with students who have puzzled about how to begin their writing. This is because until text is written down you cannot receive the advice that you need from your supervisor about how it should develop. A few inaccuracies in an early draft can be corrected at a later stage. Trying to become a habitual writer is the best way to improve your writing skills. Ward (2000) argues that short periods of writing every day produce more and better writing than the practice of binge writing. Writing all the way through your research cannot be overstressed and one of the best places to start is in a notebook or journal. Your journal is probably the most important research tool you will possess. It will contain what is happening in your thoughts as you conceptualise ideas and confide your feelings or concerns to the journal page. Writing completed while your research is fresh will have life and verve and reflect keener insights. Getting into the habit of writing up your notes regularly is also one way of practising and refining your writing skills and will provide you with a lot of material that you can put directly into drafts of your thesis. An EdD student describes the information she kept in her research diary, such as short interviews and other comments and feelings about the research process. She describes it as a:

Researcher's diary consisting of notes of the 'five-minute informal interviews'. This included bits of infor-
mation, experiences, interactions and other miscellaneous field notes. These have been collected since the
beginning of the study in January 2002. The majority of entries in the diaries have been questions and
answers in the five-minute-interview format, although there is a considerable amount of 'free flow'
entries relating to tones, feelings and other comments which do not directly relate to the five-minute-
interview topics.

(Asong 2005: 56)

If you are unsure how to begin in your journal a useful starting point is your research questions. As you read and extend your literature review you can return to your questions and document how you see them changing as you expand your knowledge of your field. Or simply write about what is important to you and any problems you may be experiencing. The most important part of the writing process is making a beginning.

How do you know when to begin writing? Wolcott (1999) has offered the following advice:

It is time to start writing if you have not begun to write, yet you feel that you are not learning anything
sufficiently new to warrant the time you are investing. Start writing up what you already know …
   It is time to start writing if you have not begun to write but you realise that you will never get it
all and the possibility has crossed your mind that you may now be using fieldwork as an excuse for not
writing …
   It is time to start writing if you have not begun to write, but you have convinced yourself that after
attending 'only a couple more' big events, or investigating 'only a couple more' major topics, you will
begin …
   It is time to start writing if you have not begun to write, yet you realise that you are now at the
midpoint of the total time you have allocated for completing the study.

(Wolcott 1999: 199–200)

He goes on to suggest it is never too early to begin to write and argues that there are advantages to writing a preliminary draft before you even begin your fieldwork. While such a draft is likely to be only for yourself, he argues that it will propel you into the field already focused on the ultimate purpose of your research. It will prompt you to think about how you will organise your final account and what sequence you intend to follow as your research story unfolds. An early draft will help you to establish what you already know and what you need to find out. He argues that your writing will invite you to examine your own biases, assumptions and emotions and make them a matter of record in a form readily accessible for your own future use.

Thinking about how you structure your work will also help you to begin writing. Learning to recognise the difference between what are distractions to starting your work and what are legitimate warm-up activities can be helpful. Ward (2000) suggests that there is no single right way of warming up. There is only one definite wrong way – when you do not achieve your writing target. The best way to warm up is by writing, while telling yourself that your writing will get better as the day progresses. He suggests the use of writing prompts such as 'Somewhere in my thesis I need to say something about ...' just to get you going. He also recommends the work of Murray (1984), who proposes a number of ways to start writing, a few of which are given below.

- **switch your writing tools;**

- **write down the reasons why you are not writing;**

- **describe the process you went through when a piece of writing went well;**

- **make writing a habit;**

- **call the draft an experiment or an exercise;**

- **dictate a draft.**

Writing down exactly what you hear in your research setting and during the collection of data can provide you with rich information. Such comments may help you to put your ideas onto paper and may become particularly important at a later date when you consider how you might analyse your data. Cheri Logan explains:

> *Early in the investigation it became apparent that the terms in which respondents discussed graphic design knowledge were distinctive and unusual. The language in which respondents shared their ideas was rich in metaphorical allusion, enabling their productive discussion of joint concerns and vivid responses to interview questions; the first challenge the research presented me with was to understand this 'idiolect', or specialised language. The second involved finding a way to represent it effectively to others, as its tacit and allusive references to knowledge seemed at odds with and difficult to represent in the formal, declarative language required to address a wider audience.*

(Logan 2005: 78)

Cheri Logan began her writing process through keeping careful notes about what exactly respondents said so that she could identify the metaphors that they used in their work to understand the 'specialised' language of her respondents. In doing this she also began to make decisions about the structure of her thesis, which is the theme of our next section in this chapter.

Deciding the structure

Making a decision about structure can be the single most important thing that can give you the momentum to move forward. In writing your initial proposal in order to gain a place on a doctoral programme, you will already have begun to form ideas about the structure and shape of your thesis. You will have considered some of the literature, thought about your research methods and methodology, and decided what might be the most suitable approach to researching your topic. Refining and developing this early proposal will help you to begin to think how the parts might join together to make the whole. Having a more detailed synopsis will enable you to estimate the number of words in each section of your thesis so that you can break down your thesis into manageable chunks and this will free you to start writing from any point.

Perfection of design in your structure for your thesis is not possible – it will always be flawed. This is because while your ideas will be multidimensional the structure of your thesis is linear and unidimensional. However, making decisions about the structure of your thesis may be perplexing and there are several questions you will want to address. What kind of context should you provide? Should you present your data in terms of themes, structure it chronologically or by what is perceived as most important? How should your literature review be structured to reflect what will come later in your thesis? These are questions all researchers have to face. When writing his PhD, Becker (1986) could not decide whether to offer his readers a background discussion of the types of school first and then present his findings about relationships or, alternatively, to discuss his major findings on relationships first and then look at differences in types of school. Becker's conclusion was that there was no one right way. Writers have to choose a way that works for them, a structure they can justify, and then get on with it. This is what you have to do. Decide on a structure you can justify and then begin writing.

Setting targets

Start at the end and work backwards is the advice most professional writers give. In order to complete the project it is necessary to produce the right number of words in the right place and at the right time. In order to do this you need to set yourself targets. Writers need to construct manageable word targets for themselves each day, week, month and year. Targets also need to include how much time to set aside for revising, correcting and editing drafts. Many aspects of the writing process will take longer than you think, such as getting feedback, making minor revisions, compiling a bibliography, checking references, checking figures, completing the preliminary pages (acknowledgements, contents page, abstract, etc.) and checking details of the bibliography. This is one of the reasons why it is important to stick to your structure and write an early first draft.

Setting writing targets is linked to effective reading and involves:

- **choosing something to read that you can write about;**

- **asking the right questions about what you want from the reading;**

- **making your reading work for you in your writing.**

If you look back at Chapter 3 on Developing a Literature Review you will find much advice about tackling your reading.

Reading is intimately linked to the writing process. It is not possible to remember all that you read and so it is important that you have a way of recording the literature. On each occasion you should ask yourself – 'Where will this reading fit into my thesis?' In one sense, some of your targets are already set by the structure of the EdD programme. Structuring and agreeing with your supervisor what the content of each draft chapter will be is a very important part of setting yourself writing targets.

Themes and concepts

Explanation of the conceptual problem of your thesis can sometimes be initiated by the use of sentences such as 'The purpose of this study is …' However, if that is the point at which you are stuck then your problem is not to do with writing but is conceptual. To resolve this situation you will need to solicit help to resolve your problem of focus – draw upon all the people resources you can for this, – especially those who you think have an analytical turn of mind. It may be that by simply putting into words your previously unexpressed thoughts you can clarify the situation.

You may also find it helpful to think of your research as a problem to be solved rather than as a fixed research question. What are the questions that you need to set yourself in order to solve your research problem?

One of the questions you will need to address is the theoretical basis of your research problem. What are the theoretical implications of your work likely to be? This is a problem you cannot shy away from in a research thesis and it has important implications for how you develop and write up your literature review and your analysis of data.

Wolcott (2001) argues that you should introduce theory when it is quite clear what you are interested in theorising about and how that relates directly to what you have to report. He considers this to be a linking activity and warns against premature excursions into analysis or interpretation. He says:

> *This is not to suggest that the lines between description, analysis and interpretation are so clearly drawn, but only that you keep the focus on the descriptive task until you have provided a solid basis for analysis and for determining how and how much to draw on the work of others.*

(Wolcott 2001: 75)

The theoretical interpretation that you write into your data should mirror the complexitiy of trying to do this rather than try to infer a single 'real' meaning. Woods (1985) indicated a number of ways in which writing is sometimes theoretically inadequate and suggests some forms of this that you should try to avoid in your writing:

- *Exampling:* **all that is done is to provide illustrations of someone else's concepts or theoretical constructs. What you should try to do is re-examine the data carefully and say what else they reveal through asking questions such as: How can the data be tested or falsified? What considerations are omitted? How adequate are they as representations of data?**

- *Theoretical lag or mismatch:* **this may come about through being previously steeped in certain methods and approaches and the difficulty of breaking the mould and viewing the world otherwise.**

- *Under-theorised description:* **this is little more than the presentation of the data as they stand without attempting to analyse, explain, draw out common features across situations and identify patterns of behaviour. It may be good journalistic writing but it is inadequate as academic research.**

How one EdD student identified the themes in her research is explained in the following two extracts from her analysis log:

9.9.03
Worked on [analysis of Interview 12] last week and now on his [Tutor B's] second theme, techniques and skills. Need to note that my method is to go back through the 'cut & paste' segments on a theme, trying to identify sub-categories or sub-themes (e.g. 'the representation of ideas', 'the structures of thought' etc.). I'm also looking for key metaphors that represent these themes, but increasingly I'm finding that there's a reciprocity and that the metaphor use also helps identify the themes. So, onto skills and techniques ...

15.10.03
It is very significant that my analysis log ended where it did, i.e. 21.9.03. At this point (and until 24.9.03) I was pursuing metaphorical analysis successfully. Then I started to do emergent theme analysis on Observation (23) and completely lost track. I was panicky about [the next progress report] PR08. Now I have to relocate my method. I have re-read all the interview (12) metaphorical analysis, and I also need to look at all the earlier stuff – the other tutor first round interviews, the two teaching observations for the editorial specialism and 'Fanzine', and the two student interview responses (interviews 15 & 18). I'm going to see if I can reassure myself by spending the next hour looking at the material and seeing if my 'master' metaphors can go into 'families', as [my supervisor] suggested.

(Logan 2005: 185)

An important part of the research process is drawing theoretical implications out of your own data. However, advancing theoretical knowledge is not a step every researcher can make. Pointing the way for others or adding to the accumulation of knowledge is just as important. If you present your account well and offer what you can by way of analysis and interpretation you will be making your research accessible and fulfilling your obligation as a researcher and writer.

Style issues

What style of writing to adopt puzzles many EdD students as they usually have a personal and professional link with their research studies and yet want to present their data in the formal, traditional way adopted by doctoral students in the past. The choices are to write in the first person, in the third person or to adopt the passive voice. Writing in the third person is often used when the research is quantitative in nature and the researcher wishes to adopt a stance that is entirely objective and distanced from the research. However, the expectation of a reflexive approach from doctorate in education students who are studying an aspect of their professional practice or personal career development can make the use of the third person difficult to employ! Many EdD theses are written in the first person as this allows the researcher to explain choices that have involved subjective and personal decisions about the direction the research process has taken and the different changes in emphasis. The use of the passive voice where the writer might state 'It was decided qualitative research would be appropriate to explore the research question ...' is a formal style that can also be adopted in doctoral research. The style that you choose therefore will be linked to the nature of your research and the processes that you need to describe in the collection and analysis of your data. However, as Blaxter et al. (2001) suggest, you would be well advised to check out your writing style with your supervisors as you would not wish to have to do a lot of reworking or to have your thesis rejected purely on the way it was written up.

There is an expectation that the language you use will be non-discriminatory and gender neutral. Guidance on how to express yourself in this way is often provided by the institution in which you are studying. The main issue is to avoid confirming particular stereotypes by the use of 'he' or 'she' where this is not appropriate. This problem can often be avoided by employing the plural. The key principle to bear in mind is that your writing should not denigrate or exclude certain groups of people on the basis of sex, age, race, religion or other physical characteristics.

How references and quotations should be managed as part of a writing style often hinders doctoral students in their writing process. It is important here to state that you should look at the rules and regulations of your own institution on how you should style referencing and quotations in the writing up of your thesis as you may be required to use a particular system. Managing your literature searches carefully will help you to retrieve information quickly when you need it.

As your research progresses, you will find it increasingly difficult to remember what you have searched and what you have found. It is advisable to establish a system early on for managing information. You will need to record bibliographical details for making references or citations, and also for jogging your memory about the content and usefulness of what you have read. It may sound a chore to do this – it is tempting to leave the organisation of your material until the end because it does not seem a priority. However, having information to hand can save much time at a later stage, when you really need that time for writing or reading, not for trying to find a piece of information you have mislaid. It is also important to keep a record of all the items you have looked at, whether useful or not. Later you may come across a reference to something you have already rejected and having a note of why you rejected it will avoid wasting time obtaining it again – long after you have forgotten why it was not of use or that you have read it before.

There are a number of ways you can record bibliographic details, abstracts and notes, but it is important to choose a system that suits the way you prefer to work. Bell (1999) gives particularly helpful advice on note-taking and recording information. For example, a manual system using notebooks or index cards is cheap and easy to carry around and you can transfer the information on to your computer's word-processing software to create a bibliography that you can edit, and copy to paste into your work. Bibliographic software packages help you to store and organise your references to books, journal articles and other materials. You can download references/records direct from many bibliographic databases, then search and sort your own references to generate bibliographies.

Follow a consistent style for maintaining your own file of bibliographic references. When citing material published some time ago but accessed by you in a more recent edition you should make sure you indicate the edition used. Remember that your examiners and other readers will consult your sources and you owe it to them to be accurate and complete.

The final stage is the easiest although it may not feel as if it is. At this stage you will still need to be aware that you may have some problems with structure but it will largely be a matter of reformulating sections that you have written to make them more effective. You will need to add detail, more evidence to fill out the argument and move paragraphs and sentences so that they are placed more effectively. While these activities may seem tedious, they are worth the final effort and can make all the difference between an adequate thesis and a good thesis.

Using the right words for what you wish to say is more than simply a matter of good communication. The words you use carry implications for the phenomena you are writing about. You should also try to get your grammar and spelling as sound as possible and not just rely on the spell-checker on your computer!

Negotiating feedback

Writing with feedback is the most powerful way to improve your writing. However, many people find it difficult to accept critical comments and become very defensive. Elbow (1998) writes that:

Thorough revising relies most of all upon time – more time for careful wrestling and more time in addition for setting your writing aside, which gives you newer, fresher eyes than you could get by mere will power or any vow to be dispassionate. Cut-and-paste revising ... relies on aesthetic intuition. When you revise with feedback you are of course trying to use all these faculties, but in addition you are using the most powerful tool of all: the eyes of others.

(Elbow 1998: 139)

There may be many reasons why students do not ask for feedback or act upon it when they receive it from their supervisors. If you are in a hurry you tend to hold off the feedback until the end as you do not really want to make any changes. If you follow this style of responding to feedback the effect on your writing is negligible as you can make only very minor or cosmetic changes. If you use feedback early you can use the reactions of others as part of the process of making up your own mind. Where you have not received feedback that you can act upon in your previous academic work it may be difficult to understand just how helpful it can be. Listening to other research degree students' reactions can be a valuable way forward. One PhD research student comments about her supervisor:

She finally rescued me from my abyss by writing me a pretty straight letter. The gist of this was why the hell did I think I could manage on my own and why didn't I come to see her for regular supervision which, in her experience, students always needed. Since that point I think I have gradually learnt how to use my supervisor to help me. It's not easy. I have to tell her what I need to do, e.g. Please remind me that at the end of the month I will write a summary of what I am going to do next. It is almost like using someone to be an extension of oneself. So all the emotions that I feel about my work: e.g. Guilt about the slow progress, fear of failure, sudden loss of confidence, are felt more acutely during supervision. I don't find it easy to make and keep appointments, I get anxious. But this is the necessary tension which then means I can creep slowly forward after each session.

(Salmon 1992: 88)

Another research student's account of her feedback from her supervisor goes as follows:

From the beginning, she challenged, always pushing my boundaries, moving me towards regions that often threatened. Challenging me to be more reflexive about myself as a researcher and where and who I was in relation to the research. To find my own voice and express it. To show explicitly how I was being challenged and changed through the journey of the research. Helped me to understand from the inside out, a key validity concern in qualitative research ... If she had merely facilitated me, been responsive to my needs, I could not have learned as much as I did, nor would I have had such courage to push back my boundaries. Challenged me to move beyond my own givenness. And in ways that involved the whole of me, not merely my intellect.

(Salmon 1992: 97)

Working with your supervisor and keeping in touch throughout all the processes of your research is essential as the comments from research students reveal. Learning to work with your supervisor is a difficult process and this is why we have discussed this issue early in the book (see Chapter 2). As an experienced writer, your supervisor is there to challenge your writing, to advise on how to develop it and express your ideas in new ways.

Conclusion

We have tried to demystify some aspects of the writing process and hope that to some extent we will have succeeded! In the end, the way to learn is to read, write and study the end product of writers you respect. Who are the role models for you in your subject? Try to find people who inspire you. Go to places where writing is discussed and take part in conversations with other writers and researchers. Above all – write!

10 The Examining Process

Here we look at the final and challenging hurdle you have to overcome before you will be able to use the title 'doctor' in conjunction with your surname. In this chapter we are concerned with making your findings public by submitting your thesis to scrutiny by others, usually respected fellow academics with an interest in your chosen field. Students at this final stage of the process often have practical questions in mind. The 'how' is often more pressing than the 'why'. How do I submit my thesis? What will the examiners look for when they read my thesis? How do I prepare for the viva? These are the kinds of questions this chapter seeks to answer. It will look at:

- **submitting your thesis;**

- **what the examiners are looking for;**

- **preparing for the viva;**

- **achieving results.**

Submitting your thesis

The final stage is about preparing to step out and become visible. In other words, reading, collecting and analysing data as well as writing up findings is in many respects a very personal and private affair between you and your supervisor; now you are faced with having to let others make judgements about what may have taken you a long time to complete. Some may argue that doctoral studies can be experienced as mysterious and mystifying (Morley et al. 2002). But do not forget, presenting your findings and submitting to a viva offers you the chance to 'show off', to explain to others that what you have achieved is really significant and hence worthwhile to be offered to the wider research community. The whole process can therefore be a very positive experience – and for most students it often is! Before going into further detail, let us look at some of the practical issues.

There are three stages to the examination process:

- **submitting your thesis;**

- **the oral examination (the viva);**

- **dealing with the examiners' recommendations.**

Submitting your thesis involves understanding institutional policies and requirements in relation to (a) the whole examination process, and (b) the submission of the
thesis itself. Here students are advised to be particularly conscientious. Bear in mind
that there will be general guidelines which apply to all research degrees according to
the *Code of Practice for the Assurance of Academic Quality and Standards in Higher Education*
issued by the Quality Assurance Agency for Higher Education (QAA 2004) adopted
by your institution, and to specific course-related ones which are relevant to your
research. Guidelines offer a kind of safety net, a list of dos and don'ts, of rights and
responsibilities to all those involved in the examination process in addition to examination criteria that have to be fulfilled. When you are at this stage in your thesis
remember the following:

- **play the game according to specified rules!**

- **check that you have all the paperwork needed: regulations, guidelines, papers
  giving advice on the examination process (administrative criteria);**

- **ensure that you understand the status of results and what these may mean for
  you in practice;**

- **read and digest all guidelines and regulations given to you – not just a few;**

- **ensure that you fully understand the precise wording of assessment criteria and
  discuss these with your supervisor.**

When presenting your thesis:

- **stick firmly to guidelines concerned with the presentation of your thesis (the
  number of words required, the referencing system required, advice concerning layout, abstracts, page referencing, what to include in appendices, binding and so on);**

- **avoid spelling errors, poor punctuation and errors in syntax, incomplete tables, etc.**

Many examiners are negatively influenced by a poor presentation of the thesis, even if its content is relevant and exciting. Mullins and Kiley (2002) found in their research that with most examiners 'first impressions count'! Examiners (in common with most teachers) hate 'sloppiness' in calculations, referencing, or typographical errors. If there is sloppiness in presentation, then the thinking is that the analysis of data, for example, might also be sloppy.

> *These first impressions were not irreversible, but they did influence the examiner's frame of mind for the rest of the thesis. Experienced examiners decide very early in the process whether assessment of a particular thesis is likely to be 'hard work' or 'an enjoyable read'*

(Mullins and Kiley 2002: 377)

However, while all of this may seem simple and straightforward, research undertaken on the examination process itself indicates, perhaps not surprisingly, that it is full of ambiguities and complexities. Trafford and Lesham (2002) point out that while examiners are looking for a range of scholarly and academic criteria in the examination process, the adherence to administrative guidelines also matters. Again perhaps not surprisingly, candidates do not always take full advantage of such criteria, guidelines and supervisory advice! Furthermore, there is as yet no consistent body of knowledge which could assist examiners in the job of examining. Instead, there is an abundance of anecdotes, sometimes of a traumatic kind, which can add a sense of drama to the whole process. Increasingly, however, examining institutions offer induction and training courses, workshops or seminars to internal and external supervisors and examiners in an effort to standardise the process of examining.

What the examiners are looking for

So far we have only looked at relatively straightforward and fairly obvious aspects of the examination process. The following discussion will be more complex. There are two kinds of assessment criteria to be considered – the explicit, transparent ones which are framed in the language of guidelines, rules and regulations, and the implicit, less easily accessible ones such as 'coherence', 'critical understanding', 'logical development of arguments', 'relevance to practice', among others, that are embedded within the thesis itself and are reliant on the perception of individual examiners. 'Relevance to practice', for example, is particularly significant for professional practice-based doctorates which present enquiries by professionals concerned with teaching and learning in education and other areas of work (e.g. nurses, police and civil servants). It is important therefore that examiners, who may have more experience with examining PhDs, understand that a thesis for a professional doctorate will be different and cannot be judged solely according to PhD criteria. For example, PhDs are usually longer (about 100,000 words), which means that theoretical discussions can offer more breadth than is possible in a thesis for a professional doctorate, which is generally much shorter (about 50,000 words, depending on institutional regulations). On the other hand, discussions in an EdD thesis are often more focused and less prone to digression. Furthermore, the data gathered for a professional doctorate may not be as comprehensive when compared to a PhD, though the level of critical analysis and evaluation should be the same. It is important therefore that examiners are given all the necessary information which allows them to understand a professional doctorate thesis fully before they begin scrutinising it in detail.

There are other points to consider. Some examiners, for example, have a preference for a more traditional approach to the sequencing of chapters (introduction, literature review, methodology, followed by data collection, analysis and evaluation) while others do not mind a more varied and flexible approach. Some may have a personal preference for the presentation of quantitative data in the positivist paradigm; they may feel less comfortable with a biographical approach and interpretation though most will accept a wide range of research approaches. The selection of examiners, therefore, involves a range of considerations. Tinkler and Jackson (2004) advise on the selection criteria for doctoral assessment as follows:

- Assessment of thesis – shaped by the examiner's expertise, academic approach (including willingness to accept alternative approaches) and personal/political agenda.
- Content and conduct of the viva – shaped by the examiner's assessment of the thesis, examiner's expectation of the candidate's knowledge, examining style and interpersonal dynamics in the viva.

(Tinkler and Jackson 2004: 69)

Bear in mind that you are by now the expert in your own area of research, and not necessarily the examiner, although the latter should nevertheless be an authority in your field of research and someone whose comments you would therefore value. Furthermore, you may want to have an examiner who has a positive approach and is sympathetic to you as a candidate and will understand your initial nervousness. These are matters for you to discuss with your supervisor before examiners are appointed.

Increasingly, examiners will undergo some kind of training or briefing organised by the candidates' institutions so that they are fully familiar with the examination process and its regulations. Once appointed, examiners are usually required to submit a formal report or an evaluation of the thesis in advance of the viva. In other words, they will have drawn at least preliminary conclusions before the viva takes place.

While the wording of (academic) assessment criteria will vary from institution to institution, Winter et al. (2000) show that examiners of doctoral theses, from across disciplines, ask questions that display a pattern of consistency. Their evidence is that examiners focus on the following critical factors:

- **conceptual clarity in the design, conduct and analysis of the research;**

- **intellectual appreciation of how underlying theories relate to issues in the research;**

- **engagement with the literature;**

- **grasp of methodology;**

- **coherence of argument;**

- **presentation of the thesis and compliance with academic protocols.**

Most criteria will include the notions of originality, criticality and, within the context of a professional doctorate, relevance to practice. The term 'original' as discussed previously is, of course, a negotiable concept. Nevertheless, it assumes that research findings will offer something 'new' to the professional and scholarly community. Often candidates fail to make this aspect clear enough in the final chapter of the thesis. There is a temptation to understate achievements, to assume that readers will come to that conclusion of their own volition. So beware, be explicit and proud of your achievements, and confident that they are worth reporting.

The assessment criteria

The precise wording of assessment criteria will vary from programme to programme and from institution to institution. There are four criteria used for the assessment of an EdD thesis in The Open University. One criterion states: *makes a significant contribution to the theory and practice of education.* The key word here is 'significant', which is, of course, difficult to define or assess, as one of the examiners indicated:

'Significant' is not a very precise word. If strictly interpreted, it could be used to justify the application of impossibly high standards. I assume this is not the intention and that what is meant is that the candidate's thesis should make more than a minimal contribution to the theory and practice of education.

(OU Examiner, Co-ordination Exercise 2004)

The problem for the examiners here is to determine whether sufficient contribution to the practice of education has been made. If the examiners are seriously concerned about this and feel that the thesis is unduly lightweight in this respect and this criterion has therefore not been met, they may well feel that they need to recommend that the thesis be resubmitted with 'substantial amendments', as identified by the examiners, and to be completed within a period of twelve months. The resubmitted thesis would then normally be checked, and if satisfactory signed off, by the internal examiner alone or working with another member of the Examination and Assessment Board.

However, bear in mind that you are not expected to be a Nobel Prize winner (Mullins and Kiley 2002). In the words of Winter et al. (2000):

All research, including doctoral research is about getting knowledge, and indeed, getting better knowledge. The 'better knowledge' in two senses of 'better': knowledge which is reliable and unbiased; and knowledge which can be used wisely, to a good purpose.

(Winter et al. 2000: 27)

The authors also state that the salient terms here, 'reliable', 'wise', 'good', are always in question. Perhaps a good point to note is that an EdD thesis should not just be about the creation of 'new knowledge' but about offering new insights in an effort to improve practice.

The notion of criticality causes anxiety among many students. Another Open University criterion states: *exhibits a high level of critical analysis*. Again it is open to a wide range of interpretations. As one examiner states:

'High' is a similar criterion to 'significant', above. I assume that what is meant here is a well-developed ability to engage in sustained critical analysis. We do normally expect researchers to develop, justify and use a theoretical base to their work. The lack of use of the developed theoretical base in the process of analysis could be a topic to be probed at a viva.

(OU Examiner, Co-ordination Exercise 2004)

There are, of course, other criteria to be considered, though it is not the intention to discuss all of these here. In any case these will vary from institution to institution. However, a further assessment criterion examiners have to consider in most institutions, particularly for a professional doctorate, is the notion that research findings should have relevance to practice. This notion of relevance can be summed up with a 'so what'? Examiners might think this is all very well but what has been the point of this research? Why should it be of interest to anybody else? A practical problem facing students and tutors in higher education is how to judge practice-based doctorates which represent enquiries by professional practitioners. Winter et al. (2000) argue that practice-based doctorates are context-bound in which the subjectivity of the producer cannot be eliminated. In other words, research questions arise out of practice and findings or new knowledge and understanding gained in the course of the research should inform practice. These are therefore relevant not only to the researcher but others in a similar professional field.

A further point examiners often consider relates to the question of whether the thesis (or at least parts of it) is publishable in an academic peer-reviewed journal. Publishability is a way of measuring contribution to knowledge, though there is no agreement about the quantity of published material to be expected (Tinkler and Jackson 2004). Nevertheless, examiners will ask themselves if the findings are worth reporting and, if so, whether the thesis is written in such a style that at least parts of it can be used for such purposes without too much rewriting. The important point to bear in mind is that examiners will have to be satisfied by all assessment criteria, not just a few, before passing judgement and making final recommendations.

Preparing for the viva

Almost all students worry about the viva, perhaps more so than they do about the submission of the thesis itself – understandably so. After all, adults are rarely used to having to submit to an oral examination, never mind a viva on which so much depends. But why have a viva at all? What purpose does a viva serve? Can a viva achieve more than the presentation of a thesis? Some countries with broadly similar education systems seldom have a viva. In others, notably in the USA and in most European countries, the viva is akin to a public performance, with several examiners, students and fellow researchers present. In Britain, however, in almost all instances the viva remains a compulsory and relatively secret part of the examination process. The viva process, therefore, remains under-researched and open to in-depth scrutiny and criticism (Morley et al. 2002). Yet irrespective of such concerns the viva is, for the time being at least, the final stage of the examination where binding decisions are made about the grade to be awarded. Furthermore, candidates do not have a great deal of scope to appeal should they be unhappy about its outcome – although all institutions have appeals procedures and you are well advised to familiarise yourself with these in advance of the viva.

One of the rationales used for the justification of having a viva is that it should serve as the authentication of a thesis. In other words, the examiners want to ensure that the candidate is the author of the thesis and that he or she has undertaken the work presented in it. Candidates authenticate their work by displaying detailed knowledge of its content, discussing methodological issues in depth, demonstrating specialist knowledge of the area and so on (Tinkler and Jackson 2004). In many institutions – but here again there are exceptions since these matters are regulated internally – it is customary that during a viva there will be a person chairing the process, either an internal examiner or someone else representing the institution. There should also be two examiners, one internal and the other one external, as well as an observer, usually the supervisor. The observer's role is to ensure that the viva itself has been conducted fairly and according to specified rules and regulations. He or she does not usually take part in the viva discussion but offers moral support to the candidate. The observer or supervisor will also want to ensure that the candidate has fully understood the grade achieved and its implications.

The viva can do several other things. It can offer candidates the opportunity:

- **to present their research to academics from outside their own university;**

- **to gain valuable professional/academic recognition;**

- **to have a stimulating and challenging discussion among equals;**

- **to explain points in the thesis which are not entirely clear to the readers;**

- **to explain gaps/misunderstandings perceived by the examiners;**

- **to locate the thesis in a wider academic or professional context;**

- **to have advice on how to improve the thesis;**

- **to have advice on where and how to publish findings;**

- **to upgrade the final grade awarded.**

While much of this may seem quite daunting, many students are surprised to find that they have actually enjoyed the viva experience they had dreaded so much. In general, examiners are not there to 'get at you'. Most will remember their own experiences, which makes them sympathetic to your situation. Furthermore, most will be genuinely interested in meeting the candidate and in what she or he has to say. There are no easy tips or guidelines for candidates to follow but they should bear in mind that the viva offers a chance to discuss and defend points raised in the thesis. Most examiners will have read the thesis two or three times. In many instances they will have produced some kind of report and they will have discussed their thoughts with the other examiner(s) in advance of the viva itself. They will have prepared some questions they want to ask. In other words, they will have spent a considerable amount of time preparing for the viva. It makes sense that candidates should do likewise.

Questions you may be asked

Most examiners will meet in advance of the viva to prepare the sequence and kind of questions they want to ask you. Trafford and Leshem (2002) have undertaken research about how vivas are conducted and the questions candidates are likely to be asked. These can be grouped into twelve clusters. These broad clusters are based, according to their research, on the following questions:

- **Why did you choose this topic for your doctoral study?**

- **How did you arrive at your conceptual framework?**

- **How did you arrive at your research design?**

- **How would you justify your research methodology?**

- **Why did you decide to use XYZ as your main instrument?**

- **How did you select your respondents/materials/area?**

- **How did you arrive at your conceptual conclusion?**

- **How generalisable are your findings, and why?**

- **What is your contribution to knowledge?**

- **We would like you to critique your thesis for us.**

- **What are you going to do after you gain your doctorate?**

- **Is there anything else you would like to tell us about your thesis which you have not had the opportunity to tell us during the viva?**

Such questions, according to Trafford and Leshem (2002), serve two purposes. First the questions may build upon the strengths to extend the ideas, models and conceptualisation that appear in the text itself. Secondly, the examiners may wish to satisfy themselves that the candidate understands and appreciates the wider significance of their research. Indeed, Trafford and Lesham suggest that the whole research design and thesis could be developed along these key questions.

This is how one EdD student, Hilary Bennison, had prepared herself for the viva:

> *I prepared for the viva by initially reading some books and articles on the viva process … I also reminded myself about the criteria that the examiners will be using for the EdD. From these sources I concocted a list of about 20 possible questions which I might be asked. I then re-read my thesis, summarising the key arguments or issues in each chapter, and answering each of the 20 questions. Finally, I listed the main authors whom I had quoted in the thesis and summarised the theories that they had written about.*

As you can see, preparing for a viva is time-consuming if done properly.

Consider the following advice given to doctoral students preparing for a viva at The Open University:

> *The further area you need to think about is the actual thesis itself and the arguments which structure it. Bear in mind that you are the expert because you wrote it. However, it is easy to forget details and even to muddle up the argument. So the next piece of advice is to make a detailed and concise summary sheet of the thesis and its structure.*

(OU EdD Research Seminar)

Another area of advice concerns the presentation. This is very important because examiners may consider, for example, that a part of your thesis is weak or that there is something you have not explained properly or that there is a contradiction between two different ideas. However, if you are able to give a robust defence, they may then conclude that you have justified it adequately, and will not ask you to make corrections. This is not easy to do because your examiners will in most cases be more experienced in this type of argument, and furthermore, as examiners, they are in a more powerful position than you. It may be worthwhile to go through your thesis and identify areas that you feel are potentially weaker than others and to think through ways and means of defending them. This will involve trying to anticipate the areas on which your examiners may focus.

You should also think about what you might have done differently. Often examiners appreciate succinctness and reflexivity, i.e. recognising both what can be claimed but also the limits of that claim. Examiners often ask what you might have done differently with hindsight and will be suspicious of those who claim they would have done exactly the same.

To sum up:

1   In answers to the questions from the examiners, you should allow yourself the time to give a full account of what you are trying to say. Do not feel rushed.

2   There is nothing wrong with engaging examiners in an argument. In other words, do not feel that because they are examining you, you cannot contradict them. This is part of the process – within reason, of course.

3   You know your work better than the examiners; do not hesitate to remind them of other parts of your thesis which are relevant, even if they are referring only to one particular part at the time. In other words, do not feel you have to just answer the question – try to expand where appropriate. Do not hold back!

4   If you are asked a question which either needs clarification or you do not fully understand, do not hesitate to ask for explanation. You may be asked questions that are poorly constructed, and it is the examiners' fault, not yours.

5   Engage with the examiners in an intellectual conversation.

6   If you are asked to make amendments, make sure that you have a clear understanding of what it is they want you to do. Your supervisor should be able to help you with this. In any case, you are entitled to written feedback from your examiners.

Achieving results

It is likely that you will have achieved a preliminary pass, with the recommendation that you either make minor or major amendments within a given time period. In common with PhDs, results are declared on the basis that there is a

- **full pass without amendments;**

- **resubmission with minor amendments (this often means that no further viva is required);**

- **resubmission with major amendments (which may or may not involve another viva);**

- **a fail (with possible resubmission, depending on the regulations of the institution).**

Bear in mind that very few candidates pass outright, so do not be disappointed if you do not belong to that exception. In some cases candidates are asked to check spelling errors, errors in syntax or referencing only, in others it may mean the rewriting of a chapter for the sake of clarification or strengthening of an argument. Examiners may feel that perhaps there are too many descriptive passages which could be shortened while the data evaluation and reflective chapters might need extending. Quite often it is the final chapter with relevance to practice that is the weakest one, mainly because candidates have run out of steam!

Consider the following: an EdD student, we will call her 'Marion', had presented a thesis around work-based learning. Her main instruments for data collection were observations and interviewing. In addition, Marion had compiled a research diary and analysed numerous documents. Following her viva, she was asked to make 'major amendments'. She had failed to make the way she went about analysing her data transparent to the examiners. In other words, Marion had given a diligent account of how she collected the data and then written a chapter about the evaluation of her data, but missed the vital step in the middle of the process, that is, explaining how she had set about analysing the data she had collected. Furthermore, she had included very little data – not enough as far as the examiners were concerned. While the examiners were complimentary about the topic and the approach she had chosen, they felt that in the end she had not done herself justice, and that the data she had presented did not really reflect the amount of work and effort that had gone into its collection. Her final chapter remained relatively thin. She was asked to rewrite both the chapter on data presentation and analysis together with the final chapter on evaluation, and to include further examples of her data analysis in the appendices. Having talked through these concerns with the examiners and her supervisor, Marion felt that she could tackle the suggested amendments and conceded that the final thesis would be much improved by such a process.

The presentation of data analysis also caused problems when a student we have called 'Philip' submitted his thesis. He had interviewed teachers and students in his school. However, he had promised both groups absolute confidentiality. Problems arose when he was asked by the examiners to include fuller transcripts than the short excerpts he had included in his thesis so that the analysis of his data would be more transparent. Philip was reluctant to do so without further permission from his interviewees, which he thought might be difficult. He had not fully understood that a thesis will be made public by his institution's library! In the end, he was able to obtain permission from key people he had interviewed by agreeing to change their names and disguise some of the background information provided in the thesis.

All candidates should expect written confirmation of their result status within a specified period of time, together with detailed feedback about what needs to be done in order to get a full pass and the date by which the revised thesis has to be submitted.

Hilary Bennison had achieved a pass with minor amendments (spelling mistakes, ambiguous referencing and the odd sentence that did not read that well). This is what she said about her viva:

> The viva itself was not quite as daunting as I had expected. Both the examiners were very friendly. The external examiner gave me quite a thorough grilling, but I felt the questions he asked and the issues he raised were all very fair. Some of his questions were to do with lack of evidence for some of the claims that I was making in my thesis, and others were more to do with my literature review and why I had not included either specific authors or concepts. Some of his points I agreed with and others I felt able to challenge. The internal examiner picked out small discrepancies or inaccuracies in my text, some of which I was already aware of and all of which can easily be put right. On reflection, I was probably only asked three or four of my anticipated questions, but I still felt that the process of compiling possible questions and working out the answers was a useful form of preparation.

Some candidates will be given additional time for working on the resubmission with their supervisors; however, the arrangements vary in different institutions. Candidates should make sure they know what can or cannot be expected of their supervisor, the examiners and the institution. If for some reason they are not happy about the way the viva was conducted then they should find out what options are open to them in case they want to make a formal complaint. In almost all cases, however, complaints may be upheld only on procedural grounds and not on academic ones – here the examiners' marking is final, even if the questioning was considered to be unfair. However, while few candidates formally raise points of concern following a viva, many say how much they enjoyed the viva and how positive they had found the experience, as is indicated in the following quote:

When I did my own doctorate I found the viva the most vital experience of the whole process, as it was the first time that my work had been taken seriously as a totality and it liberated me to speak about it in ways that I had not had the opportunity previously.

(Richard Edwards, EdD Viva Advice Seminar 2001)

Similarly for Hilary, who wrote

The viva lasted about an hour but felt much shorter, and in some respects I actually enjoyed the opportunity to discuss my thesis in-depth with academic colleagues. It felt good to get some recognition of the work that I had put into the thesis, and also to discover areas of mutual interest. The viva seemed to highlight a definite transition from what had been a very personal project into a more public arena.

(Hilary Bennison 2004)

Conclusion

This chapter has set out to demystify the examination process for you and to reassure you that the process is, in the main, rigorous and fair. Most EdD candidates worry a great deal about the viva, often before they even begin their research. But then most learner-drivers worry about the driving test, or children about school examinations. Towards the end of their research, however, when the writing of the thesis is more or less completed, most candidates are proud of their achievements and keen to share their findings with experts in the field, and not just their supervisors. It is part of climbing a mountain, reaching the top and hoisting the flag!

11 Sharing Your Research Findings

Your supervisors, colleagues and your examiners will have encouraged you to give conference papers and to share your findings with colleagues and others in the professional field, before and after your viva and completion of your doctorate, that is, once you have collected and analysed sufficient data to enable you to do so. Indeed, your employers may have supported your studies, financially or by letting you have time off to study, and in return expect feedback from you on your achievements. Colleagues in your school, college or office will have shared some of your excitement and frustration with you and expect to learn from you what new insights you have gained on the basis of the data you have collected, and which are of relevance to practical issues they face. As you know, the relationship between theory, research and practice is the glue that binds the professional doctorate together. There is, however, another point to consider: while you should get recognition for your achievements, once it is all over, you will want to 'get your life back', read a novel, socialise or pursue interests you have had to ignore for quite some time. In other words, you might want to pause and ask yourself: why share findings at all? Why make the effort to prepare a conference presentation, write academic papers, perhaps a book, following several years of hard study? These are some of the points raised in this final chapter of the book. It addresses:

- **why share your findings?**

- **presenting your research at conferences;**

- **writing an academic paper for a refereed journal;**

- **continuing research.**

Why share your findings?

In order to help provide an answer to a human dilemma, we have to go back to the early questions raised in previous chapters in this book about the purposes of educational research, particularly in the context of the professional doctorate in education.

There are two ways of looking at research: in one sense, research can be a systematic enquiry aimed at informing understandings of phenomena in educational settings, and in another it can be regarded as a 'critical and systematic enquiry aimed at informing educational judgements and decisions in order to improve educational action' (Bassey 2003: 111). As you know, the professional doctorate in education is concerned with the latter. Improving educational action is part of the reason why you have chosen to do a professional doctorate rather than a more conventional PhD. This does not mean raising standards to prescribed goals set by outside educational agencies and government norms, but improving your own practice, and that of others, on the basis of new insights and understandings gained from empirical data. Kincheleo (2003) talks about living in an age of mediocrity when dreaming about 'what could be' in educational, psychological, cultural, economic and political realms is somehow undervalued and even discouraged. We seem to stay, he argues, within the bounds of the market place and the neo-liberalist agenda, to make 'students competitive in the cold new economic order that faces them' (Kincheleo 2003: 3).

Doing educational research, in his view, helps to empower teachers and thereby initiate a move towards change. It is a bottom-up instead of a top-down process with which we have become so familiar. This bottom-up process relates to your everyday activities such as teaching, lecturing or organising educational events, which enable you to provide credible answers and take appropriate action precisely because you have undertaken in-depth academic research to an acknowledged high academic level. In other words, your voice cannot easily be ignored.

In the course of your research you will have become aware of the many complexities and diverse assumptions which need to be critically evaluated and perhaps challenged. Sharing your research with others can offer different perspectives and alternative ways of doings things. So what can be done? Quite pragmatically, you can take part in workshops to talk about your findings, present your findings at conferences, write reports, and/or a book or academic papers submitted for peer review in respected educational journals. You may find that there are colleagues who share your interests and perhaps have done research related to your own. It is this common understanding that can lift you out of the daily routine.

Why not begin by thinking of your thesis together with all other collected material as a chest full of treasures, which contains numerous precious items to be used in many different ways, again and again? In other words, your thesis will contain bits and pieces which you may find useful, for example, in preparing teaching material or staff development sessions, in teaching and other forms of writing, even if it is just the odd quote, some statistics or your own data which can be used. You may have developed charts, diagrams or used audio-visual materials which can be used, often in a different but equally valid context. It is surprising how often you will be able to make use of your thesis once you start looking at it in this way.

Presenting your research at conferences

Your supervisor will have encouraged you to give conference papers on the basis of your data analysis long before the presentation of your thesis. You may already be an experienced conference presenter but it is worth thinking about why so many of us take part in conferences and why it is important that your findings are reported in this way. Conferences serve many different purposes: they may address policy issues at a macro-level and hence attract politicians, policy developers and implementers concerned with education at a national or international level. Other conferences rely on professional bodies and academic networks. Some conferences may take place at regular intervals, and it is likely that some of the participants share the same network and therefore know each other. Decide if the conference theme relates to aspects of your research and, if you are not part of this network, if it is one you want to join. Some conferences are very large and more impersonal, often with broad themes which accommodate a wide range of perspectives; others are smaller, with a narrower focus. Indeed, there are some that allow participation by invitation only. Taking part in conferences can be an enjoyable learning experience, particularly if you find scholars, researchers and practitioners who share similar interests and professional experiences.

There are obvious tips: choose the conference carefully, seek advice about the conference itself, and consider finances! Occasionally, conference organisers offer bursaries for research students, or for outstanding papers. In other words, find out as much as you can about every aspect of the chosen conference before you commit yourself to giving a fully worked-out paper or workshop presentation.

Preparing papers

Many conferences with a research focus expect participants to present a paper. It is common practice to submit an abstract of that paper in advance, which has to be approved by the organising committee. Some committees have a very stringent approval process, others are more lenient in their approach. Nevertheless, the abstract you are asked to submit should not be written in a hurry but polished to perfection. Not only can it serve as an application to a conference but also as a planning tool and an introduction to a paper for a peer-reviewed journal. Furthermore, abstracts are often published in conference programmes and proceedings.

As a planning tool the abstract should give a sense of orientation by locating the research within its field or wider context. Rather like the abstract to your thesis, it should offer a rationale for the research, aim and purposes, a brief indication of theoretical frameworks and key concepts, methodologies and methods, and a summing up of the general significance of the findings. It should have a good title and opening sentence – so that the reader is immediately curious about its likely content. It is then up to the author to prepare the paper according to pre-set requirements and in the recommended style.

Writing a paper based on your research findings can be daunting, mainly because you as the researcher have to write to unknown listeners – not unlike the author of a book who, in the process of writing, addresses potential readers he or she is unlikely ever to meet and who may not even share the same period in time. Nevertheless, there exists a bond, a form of communicative interaction, between the author and the reader, or the presenter and the listener. In other words, the writer of the paper needs to understand the audience he or she is writing to. The language used and the points clarified depend on the kind of understanding that needs to be achieved. Here are some points you might want to consider:

- **Stick to given guidelines and deadlines.**

- **Don't just copy extracts from your thesis; adjust the text according to the needs of your audience.**

- **Stimulate discussion by writing a 'dialogue' paper.**

- **Assume that your audience is knowledgeable; don't state the obvious; concentrate on what is new.**

- **If possible, rehearse your paper with colleagues in advance of the conference; accept recommendations for change, if appropriate.**

- **Don't overload what you say with detail, though some examples can be useful, and try to show how your paper is of importance to your audience.**

- **Have a clear path, with some scope for re-emphasis of key ideas. The old dictum: tell them what you are going to tell them; then tell them; then tell them what you have told them, has much to commend it.**

- **Using this structure would imply a beginning to arouse interest, perhaps telling an anecdote or two to break the ice and taking the audience into your confidence, using an outline of your paper on an OHP; a main body of your talk addressing your major points systematically, but not at undue length; and, bearing in mind that people will often be glad of a second opportunity to hear about points they may have missed and will tend to remember best what comes last, a well-signalled ending which rapidly sums up the key points and leads into a discussion phase (Bloomer 2004).**

Presenting a paper

Even if you have given a paper numerous times, you are still likely to experience stage fright, so you might as well accept that this is normal and part of everybody's routine.

A presentation that is almost too polished and glib arouses suspicion that the presenter has presented the same or a similar paper numerous times before. Conference participants are usually interested in someone who has something new and different to say. Your research falls into that category. Bear in mind that if you engage with your audience with the content of your presentation, they will focus their attention on you. In other words, focus on your content, and not on how nervous you might feel. A further advice is: know your material. This should not present any difficulties to EdD researchers who have worked with the material over months if not years and know it better than anybody else. However, there is a danger of knowing too much, and not being able to be concise. Here are a few more tips:

- **Put life into your presentation, sound interested, keep eye contact with your audience and speak slowly and clearly, so that everybody in the room can hear you.**

- **Timing is very important. In many conferences speakers are allowed no more than perhaps 20 to 30 minutes. What you leave out of your presentation can be almost more important than what you put in!**

- **Make sure that you are physically comfortable, know the room layout in advance and check your technical equipment – but then these sorts of tips apply to all teaching and learning situations. Bear in mind that you have lots of experience and a great deal to say.**

- **Don't just read what you have written (although traditions vary). It is time-consuming and often badly done. It is much better to speak freely with a few bullet points or notes to stop you from digressing.**

- **Engage in the follow-up discussion; take constructive points on board, these will help when writing up the paper for publication.**

Writing an academic paper for a refereed journal

In the course of doing a literature review for your thesis you will have come across many articles in numerous journals which are 'peer reviewed' before publication. Furthermore, by the end of your study you should be able to write in the appropriate academic style and level of critique expected of publications at this level. Most importantly, you have something to say! You have collected and evaluated data that is judged by your supervisor and examiners to be really important and worthwhile. You have undertaken the literature review and considered methodology. In other words, you have done almost all the work needed for submitting one or more articles for publication.

Choosing your journal

Before you begin drafting your article, do your market research. Academic journals have a distinct readership and often a particular house style. So you need to consider their audiences and markets. Ask yourself, what journal will be right for what I want to write? What is its audience? Is it published by an academic interest group or a research network? Have I cited any articles from that journal in my thesis? Is the journal addressing a professional group such as teachers, health care professionals, staff developers and trainers, or educational researchers? What is likely to interest this group of readers? Does the journal specifically aim to reach an international audience? If so, how does this affect my contribution? There are other points to consider: does the journal have a particular bias, that is, do its editors aim, for example, to attract research articles which are devoted to critical theory? Some journals place considerable emphasis on empirical research and expect that authors give proper consideration to research methods and methodologies, others focus more on contexts and content and are less devoted to methodological points. Bear in mind what reviewers or readers of the journal are likely to know and what is new. For example, don't write a lengthy description of observation as a research method. Assume that the reader knows enough about it, and would be more interested in finding out how you have applied the methods and the outcomes you are discussing. However, the quality of the journal and its recognition among peers depends largely on the reviewing process. In some instances only the editor will make decisions. Some journals ask for 'scholarly' contributions, although what is meant by the term is open to different interpretations. Professional journals which have a practice focus may be equally as influential as prestigious research journals but count for less in the research selectivity exercise (RAE) to which universities have to submit if they want to attract additional government funding. Much depends, therefore, on your own professional context and what it is you want to achieve.

Having undertaken empirical research, however, and perhaps having already achieved your doctorate means that you should aim to publish your findings in a peer-reviewed article in a respected academic journal. Research articles are usually specific in nature and written for scholars with similar interests, knowledge and experience. Authors are expected to refer to the relevant literature and research base in that area – all of which you have already done while writing your thesis. Your supervisor will also have an interest in seeing your work published. Publications written by research students enhance the reputation of the teaching institution and the supervisors, particularly when co-authored, something which is increasingly common practice. Your fellow co-author might be your supervisor, a fellow researcher or colleague from another institution. In terms of academic recognition it is customary that the lead author's name, that is the person who has contributed the most to the writing of the article (not necessarily to data collection, is first to be listed in the byline. If the amount of work undertaken is about equal, then a listing of names in alphabetical order is customary. It is really important that ground rules about who does what and when, and who gets the most credit, are established in advance of the writing process and not once the article is finished, if you want to avoid unnecessary tension, even conflict!

Converting your thesis into articles for publication

One of the more difficult aspects of writing is converting your thesis into one or more articles suitable for publication. You simply have too much material, too much data and too much to convey. Here it is best to focus on a single key message. This might be a summing up of your key findings and the main conclusions you have drawn, a kind of mini-thesis; alternatively, you might want to focus on just one aspect and develop this further by drawing on only part of your literature review and just some of the data. You may want to take points you have not developed fully in your thesis but do so in another article. It is likely that your thesis will contain about three to four peer-reviewed articles, so some of these may require additional work.

Developing a sound structure for each chapter, even part of a chapter, is just as important as developing one for your thesis as a whole. It is worth repeating that a good introduction should catch the reader's attention with a summary of key findings located in the context of your research. The egg-timer metaphor is useful here. The introduction should open up your research area, and hence be broad in content, while the discussions of the literature, methodology and methods as well as the data analysis provide a narrower focus, with the interpretation of the data and conclusions you have drawn linking back to practice and the wider professional field.

Coping with the referees

The refereeing process may seem daunting at first. However, you have had chapters of your thesis examined in considerable detail and you are therefore used to accepting criticisms and comments. Often, more than half of the articles submitted to a journal are subjected to major or minor revision before being accepted and quite a few are rejected outright. Paradoxically, it is not unusual for the same article to be accepted by a journal of similar repute without further amendments. Nevertheless, the general advice is to comply with feedback received and rework the article in the knowledge that the final product will be much improved. The whole process can be very time-consuming. Journal reviewers are usually respected scholars and researchers in their own field and they often have a heavy workload in their own organisation. They review not for financial gain or prestige but simply to support fellow academics and the professional field. Furthermore, a journal may be published only two or three times a year with a backlog of already accepted papers to consider. By the time you have reworked your paper according to the advice you have been given and you finally see it in print quite a few months, even a year or so, may have passed.

Do contact the editor if you have concerns or queries but bear in mind who is making the decision. Editors have a considerable amount of power – but so have you. You can argue that your findings are legitimate or, indeed, that you do not want to proceed and approach another journal instead. Having had your thesis examined by senior academics in your chosen area can strengthen your claim that what you have to say is of real importance. You have proved that you can write coherently, concisely and according to higher academic standards acceptable to most refereed journals. Above all, do not give up. It is nice to see your name in print and to receive feedback on hard-earned achievements. So take advantage of all your gains but be generous and share these with others for the sake of mutuality and enhanced scholarship.

Continuing research

In the process of writing chapters for your thesis you will have come across numerous points you would like to have developed further had you been allowed the time and space to do so. It is inevitable that you were not able to delve into phenomena which aroused your curiosity or stimulated your thinking while working on your doctorate. Having completed your thesis should allow you to pursue some of those hunches with increased confidence. So remain curious. By taking part in conferences, writing papers and sharing ideas with others you will be able to make new connections and discover new aspects to your research which will encourage you to investigate matters further. Doing research can be addictive, as you will know. As Jarvis (1992: 246) states, 'beyond answers to questions lie more questions and answers and yet more questions lie beyond answers and these also demand answers. Learning, then, typifies the human condition and is part of the human quest – one that is bound to remain unsatisfied within the bounds of time.' These seem fittings words with which to end this chapter and this book.

Bibliography

Alridge, A. and Levine, K. (2001) *Surveys in the Social World*, Buckingham: Open University Press.

Arthur, L. (2002) Precarious relationships: perceptions of culture and citizenship among teachers of German, *Compare*, 32 (1), 83–93.

Asong, S.B. (2005) *Teamworking in Two Dissimilar Secondary Comprehensive Schools: An Account of Team Roles, Interaction and Interdependence in Action*, Unpublished EdD thesis, The Open University.

Ball, S.J. (1993) Self-doubt and Soft Data: Social and Technical Trajectories in Ethnographic Fieldwork, in Hammersley, M. (ed.) *Educational Research: Current Issues*, London: Paul Chapman Publishing.

Barnett, J. (2004) *Using Computers in the Workplace: A Study of Informal Learning and Perceptions of Computer Literacy in a Manufacturing Company*, Unpublished EdD thesis, The Open University.

Bassey, M. (1999) *Case Study Research in Education Settings*, Buckingham: Open University Press.

Bassey, M. (2003) Case Study Research, in Swann, J. and Pratt, J. (eds) *Educational Research in Practice*, London: Continuum.

Becker, H.S. (1986) *Writing for Social Scientists*, Chicago: University of Chicago Press.

Bell, J. (1999) *Doing Your Research Project: A Guide for First-Time Researchers in Education and Social Science* (Third edition), Buckingham: Open University Press.

Blaxter, L., Hughes, C. and Tight, M. (2001) *How to Research* (Second edition), Buckingham/Philadelphia: Open University Press.

Bloomer, G. (2004) *Giving a Conference Paper*, Seminar paper, EdD Residential Week-end, The Open University (not published).

Borg, W.R. and Gall, M.D. (1989) *Educational Research: An Introduction* (Fifth edition), London: Longman.

British Educational Research Association (BERA) (1992) *Ethical Guidelines for Educational Research*, Edinburgh: BERA.

Bruce, C.S. (1994) Research students' early experiences of the dissertation literature review, *Studies in Higher Education*, 19 (2), 217–29.

Bryman, A. (2001) *Social Research Methods*, Oxford: Oxford University Press.

Bryman, A. and Burgess, R.G. (eds) (1994) *Analysing Qualitative Data*, London: Routledge.

Bryman, A. and Cramer, D. (2001) *Quantitative Data Analysis with SPSS Release 10 for Windows: A Guide for Social Scientists*, London: Routledge.

Burgess, H. (1988) Collaborating in Curriculum Research and Evaluation, in Woods, P. and Pollard, A. (eds) *Sociology and the Teacher*, London: Croom Helm.

Burgess, R.G. (1984a) *In the Field: An Introduction to Field Research*, London: Allen and Unwin.

Burgess, R.G. (1984b) Autobiographical Accounts and Research Experience, in Burgess, R.G. (ed.) *The Research Process in Educational Settings: Ten Case Studies*, Lewes: Falmer Press.

Burgess, R.G. (ed.) (1989) *The Ethics of Educational Research*, Lewes: Falmer Press.

Burgess, R.G. (ed.) (1994) *Studies in Qualitative Methodology*, Vol. 4, *Issues in Qualitative Research*, London: JAI Press.

Burke, R. (1998) Changing career rules: clinging to the past or accepting the new reality, *Career Development International*, 3 (1), 40–5.

Burton, D. (2000a) Use of Case Studies in Social Research, in Burton, D. (ed.) *Research Training for Social Scientists: A Handbook for Postgraduate Researchers*, London: Sage Publications.

Burton, D. (2000b) Sampling Strategies in Survey Research, in Burton, D. (ed.) *Research Training for Social Scientists: A Handbook for Postgraduate Researchers*, London: Sage Publications.

Cabot, L.B. (2004) *The Dental Vocational Training Experience: A Transition from Novice Dentist to Competent Practitioner*, Unpublished EdD thesis, The Open University.

Calderhead, J. (ed.) (1987) *Exploring Teachers' Thinking*, London: Cassell.

Cobb, P., Gravemeijer, K., Yackel, E., McClain, K. and Whitenack, J. (1997) Mathematizing and Symbolizing: The Emergence of Chains of Signification in One First Grade Classroom, in Kirshner, D. and Whitson, J.A. (eds) *Situated Cognition: Semiotic and Psychological Perspectives*, New Jersey: Erlbaum.

Coe, D.E. (1994) Coming to Understand Ethnographic Inquiry: Learning, Changing and Knowing, in Burgess, R.G. (ed.) *Studies in Qualitative Methodology, Vol. 4, Issues in Qualitative Research*, London: JAI Press.

Cohen, L., Manion, L. and Morrison, K. (2004) *Research Methods in Education* (Fifth edition), London, New York: Routledge Falmer.

Cryer, P. (1996) *The Research Student's Guide to Success* (Second edition), Buckingham: Open University Press.

Delamont, S., Atkinson, P. and Odette, P. (1997) *Supervising the PhD: A Guide to Success*, Buckingham and Bristol: SRHE and Open University Press.

Denzin, N.K. and Lincoln Y.S. (eds) (1998) *Landscape of Qualitative Research: Theories and Issues*, Thousand Oaks, CA: Sage.

Elbow, P. (1998) *Writing with Power: Techniques for Mastering the Writing Process* (Second edition), New York: Oxford University Press.

ESRC (2005) *Postgraduate Training Guidelines*, Swindon: ESRC.

Evans, L. (2002) *Reflective Practice in Educational Research, Developing Advanced Skills*, London, New York: Continuum.

Finch, J. and Mason, J. (1990) Decision Taking in the Fieldwork Process: Theoretical Sampling and Collaborative Working, in Burgess, R.G. (ed.) *Studies in Qualitative Methodology, Vol. 2, Reflections on Field Experience*, London: JAI Press.

Foucault, M. (1972) *The Archaeology of Knowledge*, London: Tavistock Publications.

Gillham, B. (2000) *Case Study Research Methods*, London, New York: Continuum.

Glaser, B. (1978) *Theoretical Sensitivity*, Mill Valley, CA: Sociology Press.

Glaser, B. and Strauss, A. (1967) *The Discovery of Grounded Theory: Strategies for Qualitative Research*, Chicago: Aldine.

Gold, R. (1958) Roles in sociological field observation, *Social Forces*, 36 (3), 217–23.

Gomm, R., Hammersley M. and Foster, P. (2002) *Case Study Method*, London: Sage.

Gorard, S. (2002) Can we overcome the methodological schism? Four models of combining qualitative and quantitative evidence, *Research Papers in Education*, 14 (4), 345–61.

Greenwood, D.J. and Levin, M. (1998) *Introduction to Action Research: Social Research for Social Change*. Thousand Oaks, CA: Sage.

Guba, E.G. and Lincoln, Y.S. (1998) Comparing Paradigms in Qualitative Research, in Denzin, N.K. and Lincoln, Y.S. (eds) *The Landscape of Qualitative Research: Theories and Issues*, Thousand Oaks, CA: Sage.

Hamlin, J. (2004) *Gender Issues in Design and Technology in the Primary School*, Unpublished EdD thesis, The Open University.

Hammersley, M. (1992) *What's Wrong with Ethnography?*, London: Routledge.

Hammersley, M. (1996) The Relationship between Qualitative and Quantitative Research: Paradigm Loyalty versus Methodological Electicism, in Richardson, J.T.E. (ed.) *Handbook of Research Methods for Psychology and the Social Sciences*, Leicester: BPS Books.

Hart, C. (2001) *Doing a Literature Search: A Comprehensive Guide for the Social Sciences*, London: Sage Publications.

Hockey, J. (1986) *Squaddies: Portrait of a Subculture*, Exeter: Exeter University Press.

Holdaway, S. (2000) Theory and Method in Qualitative Research, in Burton, D. (ed.) *Research Training for Social Scientists: A Handbook for Postgraduate Researchers*, London: Sage Publications.

Horton Merz, A. (2002), A journey through an emergent design and its path for understanding, *Reflective Practice*, 3 (2), 142–51.

Howe, K.R. (1985) Two dogmas of educational research, *Educational Researcher* 14 (8), 10–18.

Jarvis, P. (1992) *Paradoxes of Learning. On Becoming an Individual in Society*, San Francisco: Jossey Bass.

Kincheleo, J. (2003) *Teachers as Researchers. Qualitative Inquiry as a Path to Empowerment* (Second edition), London, New York: Routledge Falmer.

Lave, J. and Wenger, E. (1991) *Situated Learning: Legitimate Peripheral Participation*, Cambridge, Cambridge University Press.

Le Voi, M. (2000) in *Responsibilities, Rights and Ethics: U500 Doing Academic Research, Section 7*, Milton Keynes: The Open University.

Logan, C.D. (2005) *The Representation of Knowledge and Expertise in the Undergraduate Graphic Design Curriculum*, Unpublished EdD thesis, The Open University.

Loughran, J., Mitchell, I. and Mitchell, J. (2003) Attempting to document teachers' professional knowledge, *Qualitative Studies in Education*, 16 (6), 853–73.

Manning, P.K. (1987) *Semiotics and Fieldwork: Qualitative Research Methods Series*, London: Sage.

Mason, J. (1996) *Qualitative Researching*, London: Sage.

McCormick, R. (1997) Conceptual and procedural knowledge, *International Journal of Technology and Design*, 7 (1–2), 141–59.

Mercer, N. (1991) Researching Common Knowledge: Studying the Content and Context of Educational Discourse, in Walford, G. (ed.) *Doing Educational Research*, London: Routledge.

Miles, M.B. and Huberman, M. (1994) *Qualitative Data Analysis, An Expanded Sourcebook*, London: Sage.

Morley, L., Leonard, D. and David, M. (2002) Variations in vivas: quality and equality in British PhD assessment, *Studies in Higher Education*, 27 (3), 263–73.

Mullins, G. and Kiley, M. (2002) It's a PhD, not a Nobel Prize: how experienced examiners assess research theses, *Studies in Higher Education*, 27 (4), 370–86.

Murray, D. (1984) *Write to Learn*, New York: Holt, Rinehart and Winston.

Odell, L. (1987) Planning Classroom Research, in Goswami, D. and Stillman, P. (eds) *Reclaiming the Classroom: Teacher as an Agency for Change*, Portsmouth: Heinemann.

Open University (2001) *Research Methods in Education: Handbook*, Milton Keynes: The Open University.

Open University (2004) *Research Degrees Prospectus (2004/5)*, Milton Keynes: The Open University.

Open University (2005) *Doctorate in Education Programme Handbook*, Milton Keynes: The Open University.

Phillips, E. (1994) Avoiding Communication Breakdown, in Zuber-Skerritt, O. and Ryan, Y. (eds) *Quality in Postgraduate Education*, London: Kogan Page.

Phillips, E. and Pugh, D.S. (2000) *How to Get a PhD* (Third edition), Buckingham: Open University Press.

Pole, C. and Lampard, R. (2002) *Practical Social Investigation: Qualitative and Quantitative Methods in Social Research*, Harlow: Prentice Hall, Pearson Education.

Quality Assurance Agency for Higher Education (2004) *Code of Practice for the Assurance of Academic Quality and Standards in Higher Education* http://www:qaa.ec.uk/

Ragin, C.C. (1992) Introduction: Cases of What Is a Case?, in Ragin, C.C. and Becker, H.S. (eds) *What Is a Case?*, Cambridge: Cambridge University Press.

Reason, P. and Bradbury H. (eds) (2001) *Handbook of Action Research: Participatory Inquiry and Practice*, London: Sage.

Redmond, P. (2004) *Outcasts on the Inside? A Case Study of the Career Aspirations and Experiences of Widening Participation Students from a Merseyside College of Higher Education*, Unpublished EdD thesis, The Open University.

Reid, H. (2004) *A Study of the Views of Practitioners, Managers and the Professional Body, on the Purpose of Support and Supervision for Guidance Practitioners Working as Personal Advisers*, Unpublished EdD thesis: The Open University.

Riddell, S. (1989) Exploiting the Exploited? The Ethics of Feminist Educational Research, in Burgess, R.G. (ed.) *The Ethics of Educational Research*, Lewes: Falmer Press.

Roberts, A. (2002) A principled complementarity of methods: in defense of methodological eclecticism and the qualitative and quantitative debate, *The Qualitative Report*, 7 (3), 1–16.

Roman, L. and Apple, M. (1990) Is Naturalism a Move Away from Positivism?: Materialist and Feminist Approaches to Subjectivity in Ethnographic Research, in Eisner, E. and Peshkin, A. (eds) *Qualitative Enquiry in Education: The Continuing Debate*, New York: Teachers College Press.

Rubin, H.J. and Rubin, I.S. (1995) *Qualitative Interviewing: The Art of Hearing Data*, London: Sage.

Rudestam, K. and Newton, R. (1992) *Surviving Your Dissertation*, London: Sage.

Salmon, P. (1992) *Achieving a PhD – Ten Students' Experience*, Stoke-on-Trent: Trentham Books.

Sammons, P. (1989) Ethical Issues and Statistical Work, in Burgess, R.G. (ed.) *The Ethics of Educational Research*, Lewes: Falmer Press.

Schön, D.A. (1987) *Educating the Reflective Practitioner: Towards a New Design for Teaching and Learning in the Professions*, San Francisco: Jossey Bass.

Schutz, A. (1970) *On Phenomenology and Social Relations. Selected Writings*, Chicago, London: The University of Chicago Press.

Scott, D. (1996) Methods and Data in Educational Research, in Scott, D. and Usher, R. (eds) *Understanding Educational Research*, London: Routledge.

Scott, D., Brown, A., Lunt, I. and Throne, L. (2004) *Professional Doctorates, Integrating Professional and Academic Knowledge*, Maidenhead: Open University Press.

Shacklock, G. and Smyth, J. (eds) (1998) *Being Reflexive in Critical Educational and Social Research*, London: Falmer Press.

Shulman, L. (1987) *Paradigms and Programs: Research in Teaching and Learning, Vol. 1*, New York: Macmillan.

Sikes, P., Measor, L. and Woods, P. (1985) *Teachers' Careers: Crises and Continuities*, Lewes: Falmer Press.

Silverman, D. (2001) *Interpreting Qualitative Data: Methods for Analysing Talk, Texts and Interaction* (Second edition), London: Sage.

Simons, H. (1989) Ethics of Case Study in Educational Research and Evaluation, in Burgess, R.G. (ed.) *The Ethics of Educational Research*, Lewes: Falmer Press.

Strauss, A. (1987) *Qualitative Analysis for Social Scientists*, New York: Cambridge University Press.

Strauss, A. and Corbin, J. (1990) *Basics of Qualitative Research. Grounded Theory Procedures and Techniques,* London: Sage.

Strauss A.L. and Corbin, J. (eds) (1997) *Grounded Theory in Practice*, London: Sage.

Stierer, B. and Antoniou, M. (2004) Are there distinctive methodologies for pedagogic research in higher education? *Teaching in Higher Education*, 9 (3), 275–85.

Stroh, M. (2000) Qualitative Interviewing, in Burton, D. (ed.) *Research Training for Social Scientists: A Handbook for Postgraduate Researchers*, London: Sage Publications.

Tesch, R. (1990) *Qualitative Research*, London: The Falmer Press.

Tinkler, P. and Jackson, C. (2004) *The Doctoral Examination Process, A Handbook for Students, Examiners and Supervisors,* Maidenhead: Open University Press.

Trafford, V. and Leshem, S. (2002) Starting at the end to undertake doctoral research: predictable questions as stepping stones, *Higher Education Review*, 34 (4), 43–61.

UK Council for Graduate Education (2002) *Report on Professional Doctorates*, Dudley: UKCGE.

Usher, R. and Bryant, I. (1989) *Adult Education as Theory, Practice and Research. The Captive Triangle*, London, New York: Routledge.

Wallace, M. and Poulson, L. (2003) *Learning to Read Critically in Educational Leadership and Management*, London: Sage.

Ward, A. (2000) The Writing Process, in *U500, Doing Academic Research Section 4*, Milton Keynes: The Open University.

Wenger, E. (1998) *Communities of Practice: Learning, Meaning and Identity,* Cambridge: Cambridge University Press.

Wengraf, T. (2001) *Qualitative Research Interviewing*, London: Sage.

Wield, D. (2000) Planning and Organising a Research Project, in *U500, Doing Academic Research Section 3*, Milton Keynes: The Open University.

Wilson, V.R. (2004) *Primary Mentors' Conceptions of Subject Knowledge in English*, Unpublished EdD thesis, The Open University.

Winter, R., Griffiths, M. and Green, K. (2000) The 'academic' qualities of practice: what are the criteria for a practice-based PhD? *Studies in Higher Education*, 25 (1), 25–37.

Wisker, G. (2001) *The Postgraduate Research Handbook: Succeed with your MA, MPhil, EdD and PhD*, Basingstoke: Palgrave.

Wolcott, H.F. (1999) *Ethnography: A Way of Seeing*, London: Altamira Press/Sage Publications.

Wolcott, H.F. (2001) *Writing Up Qualitative Research* (Second edition), London: Sage Publications.

Woods, P. (1985) Creativity and Technique in Writing Up Qualitative Research, in Burgess, R.G. (ed.) *Issues in Educational Research: Qualitative Methods*, Lewes: Falmer Press.

Woods, P. (1996) *Researching the Art of Teaching: Ethnography for Educational Use*, London: Routledge.

Index

A

abstracts 117
access, gaining 34–5
action research 60–1
advice, keeping records of 15–16
agendas for research 42
analysis *see* critical analysis;
    data analysis
anonymity 33–4, 37, 38
arguments, developing 27–8
assessment
  criteria, examination
      process 106–8
  of literature reviews 28–9
autobiographical approach 88–9
autonomy, in research 12

B

bias 77, 87–8
bibliographic details, recording 98–9
biographical interviews 75

C

captive triangle 45–6
case studies 58–60
*Code of Practice for the Assurance of Academic
    Quality and Standards in Higher Education*
    (QAA) 11–12, 103
collaboration 37–8
communication breakdowns, students and
    supervisors 13
conceptual frameworks,
    developing 48–51
conference papers 117–19
  preparing 117–18
  presenting 118–19
confidentiality 33–4
consent 34–5
constructivist research 55
contexts, in case studies 59
contracts, researchers and informants 37
counter incidents 37
critical analysis 26–7
critical incidents 37
critical perspectives 28
critical research 55
critical theory 46

D

data
  developing theory out of 46–7
  dissemination of 39–40
data analysis 80–9
  issues 87–8
  levels of 81–2
  qualitative data 82–6
  quantitative data 86–7
  reflexivity 88–9
data collection 64–79
  bounding and focusing research ideas 67–8
  combining methods 77–8
  developing a pilot study 78–9
  qualitative and quantitative research 65–7
  techniques 68–77
deductive approach, to research designs 46–7
democracy, respect for 32
disclosure, degree of 36
The Discovery of Grounded Theory 47
doctorates *see* education doctorates;
    professional doctorates
documentary evidence 77

E

Economic and Social Research Council
    (ESRC) 2
education doctorates 2–3
  data analysis 80–9
  data collection 64–79
  ethics 30–40
  examining process 102–14
  key issues 4–8
  literature reviews 19–29
  methodological considerations 52–63
  reasons for doing 3–4
  research 2, 5, 9–18
  theoretical frameworks 41–51
  writing process 90–101
email supervision sessions 15
emotional turmoil, reducing 14
environment, writing process 91–2
epistemology 54
ethics 30–40
  at research design stage 31–3
  collaboration 37–8
  dissemination of data 39–40
  gaining access 34–5

ethics *cont.*
    privacy, confidentiality and
        anonymity 33–4
    research relationships 35–7
    writing up research findings 38–9
ethnographic research 36–7, 89
evidence
    case studies 59–60
    documentary 77
examination process 102–14
    achieving results 112–14
    preparing for vivas 108–11
    submitting a thesis 102–4
    what the examiners look for 104–8
exampling 97
expertise
    development of 12
    reflected in writing 27–8

F

factual conception 46
feedback
    dealing with 16–17
    negotiating 99–101
feminist research 55
field notes 71
film-making metaphor 26
findings *see* research findings
focus group interviews 72–3

G

generalisation, case studies 60
grounded theory 47–8, 82

I

ideas, bounding and focusing 67–8
inductive approach, to research design 47
informants *see* research participants
informed consent 34–5
insider researchers 36
institutional arrangements, student
        support 14–15
interpretivism 55
interviews 72
    analysing 83–6
    ethical issues 35–6
    focus group 72–3
    structured 73–4
    unstructured 75

J

journal articles, converting theses into 121
journal reviewers 121

K

key informants 36
knowing how 43
knowing that 43

L

learning contracts 14
literature, character and forms of 23–4
literature reviews 19–29
    assessment 28–9
    boundaries of 23–4
    critical examination of articles 26–7
    developing academic writing skills 25–6
    developing an argument 27–8
    inclusion of sources 21
    purpose of 21–3
    strategies for recording key points 25
literature searches 20

M

methodological considerations 52–63
    paradigms 54–5
    qualitative or quantitative research 56–8
    research approaches 58–62
methodology, defined 53–4
moral duty, researchers 33
multi-strategy research 77–8

N

non-probability sampling 61, 69
normative theory 46

O

observation 70–2
ontology 53
originality within an EdD thesis 7
ownership, interview research 35–6

P

papers *see* conference papers
paradigms 54–5
participant observer roles 35, 70
passive voice 98
persons, respect for 32
pilot studies, developing 78–9
positivism 54
    see also quantitative research
post-positivism 54–5
Postgraduate Training Guidelines (ESRC) 2
postmodernism 55
practice, linking theory to 45–6
presentation, conference papers 118–19

privacy 33–4
probability sampling 61, 69
procedural knowledge 6
professional doctorates 1–2
   see also education doctorates
professional knowledge
   rationale for research 5
   theoretical frameworks 43–5
   through reflective practice 6, 7
publishability 107–8

Q

qualitative data
   analysing 82–3
   validity 62
qualitative research 56–8
   data collection 65–7
   ethical issues 30, 34
   see also grounded theory
quantitative data, analysing 86–7
quantitative research 56–8
   data collection 65–7
   ethical issues 30, 34
questionnaire design matrix 87t
questionnaires 75–6
questions, in vivas 109–10
quotations 27–8

R

random sampling 61
reality 53–4
records
   bibliographic details 98–9
   literature sources 25
   supervisory advice 15–16
refereed journals 119–22
   choosing 120–1
   converting theses into articles 121
   coping with referees 121–2
reflective practitioners 5–7
reflective stance, research reports 39
reflexivity 48, 88–9
relationships
   researchers and researched 35–7
   students and supervisors 13–14
   theory, research and practice 46
reliability 62–3
research 9–18
   agendas for 42
   approaches 53, 58–62
   change through 7–8
   continuing 122
   dealing with feedback 16–17
   developing a proposal 9–11
   ethical issues in 31

relationships *cont.*
   interaction with other
      researchers 17–18
   rationale for 5
   supervision sessions 14–16
   supervisors
      changing 14
      role of 11–12
      working effectively with 13–14
   time management 17
   training 2
research designs
   approaches to developing 46–7
   ethical issues 31–3
research diaries 93
research facilitators 22
research findings 115–22
   case studies 60
   presenting at conferences 117–19
   reasons for sharing 115–16
   writing for a refereed
      journal 119–22
   writing up 38–9
research methodology 53
research methods 53
research participants
   key informants 36
   and researchers
      contracts with 37
      relationships with 35–7
research proposals, developing 9–11
researchers
   and informants
      contracts with 37
      relationships with 35–7
   insiders 36
   interaction with other 17–18
   moral duty 33
respect 31–2
rules of conduct, statistical
      work 30

S

sample selection 68–70
sampling 61–2
self-completion questionnaires 75–6
shared observations 71
software packages, bibliographic 99
statistical work, rules of conduct 30
structured interviews 73–4
student support
   institutional arrangements 14–16
   team approach 11–12
subject knowledge 43
subjectivity, denial of 88
supervision sessions 14–16

supervisors
   changing 14
   engaging in dialogue with 10
   role of 11–12
   working effectively with 13–14
surveys 61–2
   see also questionnaires

T

target setting 95–6
teacher knowledge 43
team approach, to student support 11–12
technical knowledge 6
telephone supervision 15
theoretical interpretation 96–7
theoretical lag 97
theoretical sensitivity 48
theory 41–51
   developing a conceptual
      framework 48–51
   developing out of data 46–7
   linking to practice 45–6
   professional knowledge 43–5
   thinking about 42
   see also grounded theory
theory-building 42
theses, submitting 102–4
time management 17
transparency, research designs 33

triangulation 78
trust 38
truth 32

U

under-theorised description 97
universe of discourse 42
unstructured interviews 75

V

validity 62–3
video observations 71
vivas, preparing for 108–11

W

writing 90–101
   beginning 92–4
   deciding the structure 95
   negotiating feedback 99–101
   organising your environment 91–2
   as a process 90–1
   for a refereed journal 119–22
   research findings 38–9
   skills, developing 25–6
   style issues 98–9
   target setting 95–6
   themes and concepts 96–8